CIGARETTE COUNTRY

CIGARETTE COUNTRY

Tobacco in American History and Politics

Susan Wagner

PRAEGER PUBLISHERS
New York • Washington • London

PRAEGER PUBLISHERS

111 Fourth Avenue, New York, N.Y. 10003, U.S.A.
5, Cromwell Place, London SW7 2JL, England

Published in the United States of America in 1971
by Praeger Publishers, Inc.

Library of Congress Catalog Card Number: 72–134768

Printed in the United States of America

Contents

Preface

Smoking has never posed a personal dilemma for me. For one thing, I don't inhale, and I seldom smoke more than two or three cigarettes a day. Like many people, I light up a cigarette when I feel nervous, bored, or under pressure. For example, I lit a cigarette when I sat down to write this preface.

In other words, this is not a book with a cause. It is not an antismoking tract nor a how-to-stop-smoking book. I found myself drawn into the subject quite by chance. My interest developed out of another project, my book *The Federal Trade Commission,* published by Praeger earlier this year. As I researched a chapter on cigarette advertising for that book, the entire subject of tobacco began to interest me as a sociopolitical phenomenon. Smoking *is* a strange habit to have become so much a part of American life and mythology.

The more I delved into the history of tobacco the more it intrigued me. It is a history filled with a freaky variety of anecdotes and ironies, beginning with an irony—namely, that, without realizing it, Columbus, when he discovered tobacco, discovered a source of far greater riches than all the gold carried away from the New World by the Spanish conquistadors. I was fascinated, too, to learn that from the earliest times tobacco had been simultaneously hailed as a cure-for-whatever-ails-you and as a foul habit harmful to health.

My research led me down some surprising paths, one of them through the lovely garden at Dumbarton Oaks in Washington, D.C. There, Elizabeth P. Benson, curator for the Pre-Columbian Collection, steered me to some sources on the uses of tobacco among the Indians of South, Central, and North America. These included works by Diego de Landa, first Bishop of Yucatan, who wrote of the Mayans in the sixteenth century; the *Books of Chilam Balam*, which are seventeenth-and-eighteenth-century copies of early manuscripts from Yucatan; and the great works of Friar Sahagun on the Aztecs.

Then there were the phenomenal Arents Collections at The New York Public Library, which contain a rich variety of books, manuscripts, and engravings on the history of tobacco. This, the world's largest assemblage of materials on the history of tobacco, was the gift of George Arents, who was born in New York and later became one of the founders of the American Machine and Foundry Company and its subsidiary, the International Cigar Machine Company. Arents began collecting books as a hobby in 1898 at the suggestion of his great-uncle, Major Lewis Ginter, the Richmond tobacco manufacturer, who is mentioned in my pages.

I am indebted to an English visitor to the United States, Liliana Archibald, the translator and Russian historian, for drawing my attention to an excellent source for the short section of Chapter 1 on the Russian experience: Jacob M. Price's study, *The Tobacco Adventure to Russia 1676–1722*, published in the Transactions of the American

Philosophical Society, New Series, Volume LI, Part 1, 1961.

My father, Philip M. Wagner, provided some of the stuff for the chapter on early cigarette advertising campaigns, when he recalled an article he had written for the *New Republic.* Published on February 13, 1929, it was entitled: "Cigarettes *vs.* Candy. War Correspondence from a New Battle Front."

For the contemporary story, I have relied primarily on public records, government documents, press reports, and conversations with the participants in the unfolding health drama. My relations with industry representatives have been friendly: William Kloepfer, Jr., kindly extended to me the use of the library at the Tobacco Institute, where he is vice president in charge of public relations, and attorneys for several of the tobacco companies talked to me at length. Stanley Cohen, Washington editor of *Advertising Age,* opened up his extensive file to me.

In Congress, Michael Pertschuk, general counsel of the Senate Commerce Committee, who had previously worked on the tobacco story as legislative assistant for Senator Maurine Neuberger, proved a particularly valuable source. Special thanks also go to Emil Corwin, public information officer for the National Clearinghouse for Smoking and Health of the U.S. Public Health Service; to Dr. Robert H. Miller, head of the tobacco specialty crop section of the Economic Research Service of the Department of Agriculture; and to Dayton Moore at the American Medical Association, under whose direction a file of all AMA publications of recent years pertaining to smoking was compiled for my use.

Washington, D.C.
May, 1971

CIGARETTE COUNTRY

❦ 1

The Chiapas Gift

WHEN SIR WALTER RALEIGH'S SERVANT came upon his master smoking, so the schoolboy story goes, he thought the great Elizabethan was on fire and doused him with beer.

Not every schoolboy knows the story of Javier Pereira, an ancient citizen of Colombia, who visited New York City in 1956. A Colombian postage stamp commemorates the visit of the South American Indian, who was said to have been born in 1789, the year George Washington was inaugurated President. But U.S. public interest in the aged Pereira was transitory. True, the newspapers gave the toothless, scrappy, allegedly 167-year-old Indian a good run. And in the expected tradition, before he was whisked back to his native South American village, he made known the secret of his longevity: "Don't worry; take plenty of coffee; and smoke a good cigar." Señor Pereira may well have been a descendant of the jungle Americans who rolled the first rude cigarettes. Still, some contemporary Americans, alert to the ways of Madison Avenue, wondered aloud who paid for his junket to New York: Did Colombia produce coffee or tobacco or both?

Such is the stuff of the nicotian apocrypha. In the story

3

of tobacco, it is not always easy to distinguish between fact and fiction.

Smoking must surely be one of the most curious habits adopted by man—the only animal who takes smoke into his body for pleasure. The inhalation of smoke into the lungs would seem to run contrary to the intended use of those organs. And yet the practice is as old as civilization. In ancient Greece, the priestesses at Delphi enveloped themselves in a vapor of burning laurel before making their phophecies. Herodotus speaks of scattering hemp seeds on hot stones to produce an intoxicating smoke after dinner. Inhaling the smoke of aromatic herbs seems to have been practiced in ancient India, just as the smoking of opium, with its powerful sedative effect, was common from an early date in the Far East, and hemp (marijuana) has long been smoked in reefers or its essence taken as hashish in various parts of the world. Hippocrates, Pliny, and Galen were among those who prescribed drawing the smoke of coltsfoot, dried cow-dung, and other substances into the lungs as a cure for asthma and other afflictions. The therapeutic value of smoking certain plants was included in the prescription for asthma by the learned Arabian physician, Avicenna, in the eleventh century. Such agents were again prescribed by Pare in the sixteenth century, shortly before tobacco began to replace other recommended cures in a disease-ridden world.

Throughout history, men have searched their natural environment for products that would provide them not only with food and shelter but with certain pleasures and relief from pain and anxieties as well. In their search for gratification, they have experimented with things to drink, sniff, chew, swallow, or smoke—coca leaf, betel nut, tobacco, alcohol, mushrooms, poppy, hemp, and cactus plants, among others. There has probably never been a society that has not used some kind of fermented beverage or drug to ease the outrages of everyday life.

When tobacco was first brought to Europe in the middle of the sixteenth century, botanists and herbalists of the day ascribed the plant to the genus *Hyoscyamus* and, because of its narcotic quality, called it the "henbane of Peru," the "third kind of henbane," or "yellow henbane." The *Hyoscyami*, of which there are 1,800 species recognized today, include not only such poisonous plants as deadly nightshade but also such edibles as the Irish potato, the eggplant, and the tomato. Tobacco did not long remain a member of the family, since it was soon recognized as an independent genus that resembled henbane only in the way a horse resembles a zebra. Later, it was reassigned to a genus all its own, named *Nicotiana*, after one of its early promoters, the French envoy to Lisbon Jean Nicot. Nicot, who sent seeds of the plant from Portugal to the Florentine Queen Mother of France, Catherine de' Medici, can be regarded as one of the first propagandists for the use of tobacco for medical purposes. In his day, many gardens in Portugal had become hosts to the new plant from the Americas, which doctors had seized upon as a panacea for ills of a hundred kinds, and it was in that guise that he dispatched its seeds to the French court. (In time, tobacco became the courtesy weed of diplomacy.)

Some writers have advanced the theory that tobacco-smoking was known among Mongol tribes before the discovery of America, or that it was indigenous to China and the East Indies. Archaeologists also have had a share in advancing the theory that tobacco was known in ancient Europe. At different times in the nineteenth century, their delvings uncovered pipes in Greek, Roman, Turkish, Irish, English, and Danish ruins, and before the archaeologists themselves disproved such assumptions, enthusiasts were confusing the blowpipe with the tobacco pipe and certain carvings on Egyptian monoliths with representations of pipes on Mayan sculptures. In a Greek building in Constantinople, a pipe was found that the diggers said still retained the odor of nicotine. The existence of various types of elaborate water pipes in the Levant was cited as evidence that tobacco had long been familiar to natives of that area. But the hookah, narghile, hubble-bubble, and other forms of water pipe, later adopted for tobacco, originally were used for smoking *dakka,* or hemp transplanted from South Africa by Arab slave traders.

Contrary to old notions, tobacco is a purely American plant. It has been proved beyond reasonable doubt that smoking of tobacco originated, in some remote time, from the religious ceremonies of priests in the coastal regions of Central and South America. The oldest known evidence of tobacco use is found on a Mayan stone-carving at Palenque in the state of Chiapas, Mexico, adjacent to Guatemala: a bas-relief representing a priest blowing smoke through a long tube. The Palenque slab dates back to the classic Mayan period, which would put it somewhere between A.D. 600 and 900. A diminishing but still existing branch of the Maya, the Lacandon, who live in isolated regions of Mexico and Guatemala, were found by American explorers in this century to be growing tobacco in patches of cleared jungle, and it is now conjectured that the luxuriant jungles of Chiapas may have nurtured the first *Nicotiana tabacum,* the species most widely used in commerce today, though some authorities believe it had its ancient origin in the eastern piedmont of Peru or northern Argentina. At any rate, the use of tobacco was widespread at the time of the Spanish conquest. The tobacco of twentieth-century commerce is as American as the Indians who gave it to the world.

On October 15, 1492, Christopher Columbus wrote in his diary that three days before "in the middle of the gulf between these two islands . . . I found a man alone in a canoe who was going from the island of Santa Maria to Fernandina. He had food and water and some dry leaves which must be a thing very much appreciated among them, because they had already brought me some of them as a present at San Salvador [an island now identified with Watling in the Bahamas]."

When Columbus arrived at another beautiful island (Cuba or Haiti) a few weeks later, he sent ashore one Luis de Torres (a Jewish scholar who knew Chaldean, Arabic, and other languages and had been brought along to serve as interpreter if the explorers encountered the Great Khan) and a colleague, Rodrigo de Jerez of Ayamonte, Spain. They reported seeing natives who "drank smoke."

By 1518, the Spaniards had gone far beyond the islands they had first discovered. In that year, Juan de Grijalva led an expedition to Mexico, where an elderly Indian chief welcomed him and his band. Reporting the incident, the Spanish historian Fernandez de Oviedo says that the chief "gave the general and to each of the Spaniards . . . a little hollow tube, burning at one end, made in such a manner that after being lighted they burn themselves out without causing a flame, as do the incense sticks of Valencia. And they smelled of fragrant odor. . . . The Indians made signs to the Spaniards not to allow that smoke to be lost."

In other words, inhale, brother. Thus did the cigarette enter recorded history.

Captain Bernal Diaz del Castillo, who accompanied Cortez to Mexico in 1519, saw ornamented reed cigarettes packed with liquid amber as well as tobacco on sale in the marketplaces. Other explorers produced many accounts of pipe and reed-cigarette smoking in sixteenth-century America. But it was left to the priest Bernardino de Sahagun, a missionary a few years after the conquest, who stayed among the Mexican Indians for sixty-one years, to discriminate between the two major varieties of tobacco: *picietl*, a harsh, coarse species (which later came to be called *Nicotiana rustica*) growing in the colder latitudes, and *yietl* (*Nicotiana tabacum*), its milder, sweeter, subtropical cousin. The crude *picietl* was a poor man's tobacco. Sahagun noted that "he who sells *picietl* crushes the leaves first, mixing them with lime, and he rubs the mixture well between his hands." Even savage palates required that this coarse tobacco be mixed with lime before it could be smoked. "Placed in the mouth it produces dizziness and stupefies," the priest said. *Yietl*, the smooth leaf, not only possessed sweet-smoking qualities but gave off an incense.

The Spaniards who first explored the New World were slow to comprehend the Indian custom of chewing and smoking tobacco. Columbus and his men threw away the fruits, wooden spears, and dried leaves offered them by the Arawaks. But gradually the newcomers came to understand that tobacco was not simply an exotic embroidery on the fabric of Indian society, which enriched its myths, enlivened festivals, and gave meaning to rituals. Smoking played a part in everyday life and had real economic significance. Tobacco trade between Indian tribes had been going on for hundreds of years.

In North America, the uses of tobacco were frequent and diversified. Smoking tobacco served as a sacred act to ward off evil. The Osage Indians invoked the Great Spirit by smoking. The Sioux offered their lighted calumets to the sun. For variety, the natives of North America sometimes blended tobacco with other herbs, such as sumac leaves and the inner bark of a certain species of dogwood. By the time Europeans reached the shores of North America, the chief material used for pipes was clay, sometimes with a small bowl of copper attached to the long stem. Indian burial mounds in various parts of the United States have disclosed carved or cast pipes, some of delicate workmanship and curiously modern style.

In 1556 or 1557, one André de Thevet, a member of a French colonizing expedition to Brazil, who observed that the Brazilians believed tobacco to be "wonderfully useful for several things," took some seeds of the *yietl* back to France and planted them in his garden at Angoulême. De Thevet should probably be given credit for introducing tobacco to Europe, although others claim the honor and Nicot is the one whose name survives. The city fathers of Ayamonte, Spain, celebrate their townsman Rodrigo de Jerez as the person who first smoked tobacco in Europe. Poor Rodrigo, the same who saw the natives of the West Indies drinking smoke, was later imprisoned during the Inquisition for his "devilish habit."

For a time, most of the shops that dispensed tobacco in Europe were apothecaries. Promoters of tobacco for medicinal uses attempted to restrict its sale and deprive the smoker of his pleasure. But while the gospel of nicotine therapy (nicotine itself is the alkaloid in the plant of the genus *Nicotiana*) spread through Europe, smoking as a social habit quietly spread, too. Tobacco production expanded rapidly all over the world. By 1531, less than forty years after the discovery of America, Spaniards were cultivating the crop commercially in the West Indies; by 1560, it was being grown in Europe as an ornamental plant and for its medicinal qualities; by 1580, its commercial culture had extended to Cuba and Venezuela, and by about 1600, to Brazil. Not later than 1600 or 1605, mariners and traders had introduced it into China, Japan, South Africa, and many other countries. Holland immediately took to the "bewitching vegetable," and a brisk trade sprang up between the Antilles and the English Channel. Despite the bitter war between Spain and England, Spanish sailors smuggled tobacco into Cornwall.

British seafarers could not help but see at an early date that the brown leaf from the Americas was being converted into Spanish gold. Sir John Hawkins, who preyed on Portuguese Africa in 1562, ventured as far as the Spanish Antilles two years later and, returning by way of the Florida coast, had a chance to see and try smoking. It was probably Hawkins and his crew who brought smoking to England. Sir Francis Drake, who put in at Roanoke Island, North Carolina, and picked up the survivors of an English settlement there, encouraged the smoking habit when he returned to England. Sir Walter Raleigh created a sensation with the "witching weed" by parading his pipe before Queen Elizabeth. And although he was certainly not the first to introduce the plant to England, he perfected a method for curing the leaf and helped to popularize smoking among the well-to-do.

Smoking was an expensive pleasure: Tobacco sold for its weight in silver shillings around 1600, and indulgence in smoking ranked with dancing, hunting, and card-playing among the fashionable extravagances of London's dandies. Their display of snuff-dipping and smoke tricks, along with the excessive claims for tobacco as medicine on the part of the herbalists of the period, became the object of literary satirists and pamphleteering Puritans. The water-carrier in Ben Jonson's *Everyman in his Humour* made an observation about "roguish tobacco . . . good for nothing but to choke a man, fill him full of smoke and embers." And in 1604, King James I, down from Scotland to assume the British throne and become the patron saint of antismoking forces, anonymously published his *Counterblaste to Tobacco*. Like the educated Spanish, who at first abhorred tobacco because it was used by the barbarians of the New World, James referred to two Indians who had been brought to London from Virginia in 1584 to demonstrate smoking. "What honor or policie can moove us to imitate the barbarous and beastly manners of the wilde, godlesse, and slavish Indian especially in so vile and stinking a custome?" the king asked, and went on to mock the "smoking gallants" as a social menace. He pointed out that, in Europe, tobacco was first used as an antidote to the "Pockes" but that doctors now regarded the habit as dirty and injurious to health. The monarch's treatise concluded with a statement that smoking is "a custome lothsome to the eye, hatefull to the nose, harmefull to the braine, dangerous to the Lungs and in the blacke stinking fume thereof, nearest resembling the horrible Stigian smoke of the pit that is bottomelesse."

Had the Stuart monarch foreseen that tobacco would become the first fruit of the New World and a staple of the plantations along that lovely Virginia river which bears his name, he might never have granted charters to the adventurers determined to find their fortune on the other side of the Atlantic.

Then, again, the profit to be had from the American weed might have overcome James I's personal distaste for its use. Opposition to smoking in England was as nothing compared to measures adopted in the seventeenth century in other countries as mariners introduced tobacco to every continent in the world except Australia. (It was only in relatively recent times that seeds of a Chilean species—along with several South American sedges—got a free ride to Australia on sheep and mules. Tobacco seems to have reached the Pacific islands in similar fashion.) In Turkey, where smoking was thought fit only for the "Christian dog," offenders with pipes thrust through their noses were led on mules through the streets of Istanbul. A Chinese decree of 1638 threatened decapitation to anyone who trafficked in tobacco. More than one pope threatened offenders with excommunication. But suppressive measures did not stop smoking. They seemed only to encourage men to smoke in secret.

Russia's experience was typical. From the first, the Russian church forbade the taking of tobacco, "an abomination to God" on the Biblical grounds that "it is not that which entereth into a man that defileth him, but that which proceedeth from him." The first Romanov, Tsar Michael, forbade the sale and use of tobacco. Offenders were submitted to torture, and snuff-takers were liable to have their noses slit. A decree of 1641 mentioned exile among possible punishments. Traffickers as well as users were knouted. Financial embarrassment led Tsar Michael to violate his own law and make a fiscal monopoly of the "impious herb." Consequently, the state treasury proceeded to sell tobacco for high prices. Following popular disturbances in 1648, Michael's successor, Alexis, abolished the government monopoly and reimposed the ban on smoking. There were, however, Germans and Dutch and other foreigners in Peter the Great's new capital of St. Petersburg who did not come within the jurisdiction of the Russian Orthodox Church; and there were also some Westernizers among the Russians at court who paid little attention to the teachings of the Church. But a complete break with the past came only in 1697 when Peter the Great issued a ukase permitting the open sale and consumption of tobacco. After that, the state participated in the lucrative trade that had hitherto been conducted secretly. High import duties were imposed and a nation-wide distributive system established. Smoking rooms were soon to be found in taverns and posting stages throughout the empire.

The story was much the same everywhere. Gradually, as rulers discovered how profitable duties and taxes on the golden leaf could be, prohibitions were lifted and anti-tobacco forces were left in a cloud of smoke.

♦ 2

America's Oldest Industry

COLUMBUS FOUND THE NATIVES of America using tobacco in the forms common today—smoking, chewing, and snuff. Early records show that the Indians also understood the essential features of its production as it is now practiced, including the details of proper spacing in the field, topping and suckering the plants, and the distinctive drying processes now known as air-curing, sun-curing, and fire-curing. But it was left to John Rolfe, a youthful member of an old English family, and an ardent smoker, to develop tobacco as a staple crop, thereby ensuring the survival of the Jamestown colony in Virginia.

Rolfe left London with his wife in the late spring of 1609 on the *Sea Venture* headed for the Jamestown settlement. The ship, one in a fleet of nine, also carried Sir Thomas Gates, newly appointed lieutenant-governor of Virginia, and a number of artisans, laborers, and members of the gentry. The fleet encountered a gale, reportedly the very one that inspired William Shakespeare to write *The Tempest,* and was scattered on a Bermuda reef. All aboard the *Sea Venture* reached land safely and, out of timbers and planks salvaged from the wreck, the castaways built two new vessels. On May 24, 1610, the shipwrecked party reached Jamestown. There they were greeted by the dozen gaunt survivors of the harrowing winter known as the "starving time." Jamestown had become a graveyard for some five hundred men, women, and children, and the colony's leaders, having come to the conclusion that the colony was beyond salvage, planned to leave as soon as possible for Newfoundland. On June 7, the few remaining survivors, and the newcomers, boarded the two ships constructed in Bermuda and headed back down the James River. They had gone less than ten miles downstream when they encountered the *Virginia*. Her commander, Lord De La Warr (for whom the state of Delaware is named), was bringing 150 new settlers and more supplies. The outgoing vessels went about and returned to the abandoned settlement. They would try again.

Every effort to establish a local industry at Jamestown up to this time had failed. John Rolfe was not an experienced farmer, but he knew that the colony needed an export staple to give it economic stability. From what he had seen of the smoking habit in London, where he had himself acquired it, he believed that the logical staple would be tobacco. It could not be the type the Virginia Indians grew, *Nicotiana rustica*, which was unpalatable to English smokers. It would have to be the fragrant *Nicotiana tabacum*, which the Spanish colonists were producing in the Caribbean islands.

The two major species differ primarily in size, shape of leaves, and flower. *Nicotiana tabacum* grows from two to nine feet high, with widespreading green leaves covered with long, soft hairs containing a viscid juice, which makes the leaves moist and glutinous to the touch. Its flower is generally a light rose color. *Nicotiana rustica*, which has a flower of greenish-yellow, is a shrubby plant with small, broad, heavy leaves. Both are annuals with tiny, virile seeds, a spoonful of which will sow six acres.

Rolfe imported some seeds of *Nicotiana tabacum* and for two years tried to grow a smokable leaf. How he acquired the precious seeds remains a mystery. Perhaps one of the roving sea captains brought them from the planters of Trinidad or Caracas. The first leaves of tobacco grown from these seeds in the sandy soil of Virginia were thrown in a heap on the ground and covered with hay to help the process of fermentation. No one knows how much tobacco came out of Rolfe's first crop. Some Rolfe put aside for himself. The rest, probably no more than a few hundred pounds, was stowed aboard the *Elizabeth* for shipment to England. The dark, air-cured tobacco would resemble the coarsest, darkest type of chewing tobacco known today, but Rolfe and his companions agreed that the new leaf "smoked pleasant and strong."

In the midst of his labors, Rolfe's wife died. His romance with Pocahontas, daughter of a powerful Indian chief, flowered in the tobacco fields. The two married after Rolfe heard the news he had been waiting for, namely that expert tobacco buyers in London liked the sweet aroma and flavor of the new Virginia "Orinoco." No one troubled to keep a record of what price Rolfe's first consignment brought, but succeeding shipments sold for from five to eight shillings per pound. This was an encouraging price for a new tobacco on the London market. The news spread through Jamestown and had an immediate effect on the settlers. Colonists who had been growing corn and wheat, clearing the forests and extending the boundaries of their new community, set other jobs aside to grow the leaf that meant money.

In 1615, Rolfe and Pocahontas had a son, and the following year the family, taking along a dozen or so relatives of Pocahontas, set off for London. There, Pocahontas, who carried herself like a princess, was presented at court and became the rage of the town. Finally, wearied by the formalities and eager to return to America, she prepared for the journey home. At Gravesend on the Thames, early in 1617, when she was only twenty-two, she died—probably of influenza. Rolfe returned to Jamestown, leaving his tiny son behind in the care of a guardian.

The first great American enterprise had been launched. Jamestown became a boom town, and import duties on tobacco provided James I with an immense revenue. For a decade or more, the king continued to harass the Virginia Company, which was, he said, unable or unwilling to prevent the colonists from basing their economy on a single crop—one, furthermore, of which he disapproved. And even as late as 1622, some of the directors of the company strongly regarded smoking as a mere fad. They termed tobacco "a deceivable weed which served neither for necessity nor for ornament to the life of man, but was founded only upon a humor which must soon vanish into smoke." However, in Virginia the leaf ruled. At one time it was even grown in the streets of Jamestown.

In the colonies north of Virginia, efforts to grow tobacco were largely unsuccessful except in Maryland, where a subtype of the species was developed. It had a stronger flavor than the Virginia leaf and was cultivated along the shores of the Chesapeake Bay. But because of regulations requiring economic diversification, the settlers of Maryland did not originally make a staple of tobacco. Tobacco of reasonably good quality was also grown in the Connecticut River Valley but not in large enough quantity to export. Nor could other parts of New England, with its short growing season, hope to compete with the South. Settlers in the Massachusetts Bay Colony tried their hand at growing their own tobacco but were soon suppressed. In general, the dour New Englanders, like James I, regarded the Indians and their customs with disdain and disgust and had a distinctly blue-nosed attitude toward the creature comforts and sensual pleasures. They ventured a few statutes designed to curb use of the leaf. The seventeenth-century legal code of Connecticut associated tobacco-users with common idlers and people who hunted birds for pleasure. In 1647, the Connecticut General Court ordered that no one "under the age of 20 years, nor any other that hath not allreaddy accustomed himself to the use thereof" should take tobacco without a physician's certificate that it was "useful for him," plus a license from the court. Furthermore, tobacco could not be taken in public, or even in the open fields or woods except on journeys of ten miles or more. A citizen might smoke at "the ordinary tyme of repast comonly called dynner," but no more than two could enjoy their after-dinner pipe in the same house at the same time. The same rule applied in Massachusetts. However, Puritan antitobacco statutes were generally ignored by the colonial courts as tobacco became recognized as a home industry that needed protection. In Massachusetts and elsewhere, opposition to smoking on moral grounds was swept aside by the economic advances of tobacco. (In time, even James I came to appreciate its monetary value.)

From its modest beginning, tobacco rose to become the coin of the realm throughout Virginia and the Carolinas, justifying one of the names given it: the Golden Token. The colonial farmers who specialized in tobacco could exchange it for European products and for cash. Some made fortunes from tobacco. When the colonists asked for women to be sent out from England, their traveling expenses were paid for in tobacco. The military were paid in Virginia leaf, and the clergy found it easier to serve God in parishes where superior tobacco was grown. Ministers were known to deliver sermons on the moral virtues of proper curing. An account of tobacco-growing in Virginia was published in 1784 by an Englishman named J. F. D. Smyth, who had traveled through the American colonies as a Tory scout and spy before the Revolution and was very nearly hanged during the course of his journey. Smyth managed to fill two volumes with his observations under the title *A Tour in the United States of America.* He describes how the rich, loamy soil of the James River country produced 1,660 pounds of tobacco an acre on the best land, while the worst would yield only 500 pounds. On a trip to Westham, a small town on the James, seven miles from Richmond, he observed that tobacco was navigated down the river from the back country in hogsheads of 1,000 pounds weight each—the hogshead on two canoes lashed together. From Westham, it was taken by hand carriage to Shokoes, or Richmond, since the waterfalls prevented water transport from that point on. Smyth also wrote this description of tobacco-growing, which would not seem very old-fashioned to a Southern grower today:

As the method of cultivating tobacco in Virginia cannot be much, if at all known . . . and as a description of it may be agreeable, I shall embrace this opportunity of giving just a sketch of the manner of producing that narcotic plant which has become a commodity so beneficial to commerce.

Several rich, moist, but not too wet spots of ground are chosen out, in the fall, each containing about a quarter of an acre, or more, according to the magnitude of your crop, and the number of plants it may require.

These spots, which are generally in the woods, are cleared, and covered with brush or timber, for five or six feet thick and upwards, that is suffered to remain upon it until the time when the tobacco seed must be sowed, which is within twelve days after Christmas.

The evening is commonly chosen to set these places on fire, and when every thing thereon is consumed to ashes the ground is dug up, mixed with the ashes and broken very fine; the tobacco-seed, which is exceedingly small, being mixed with ashes also, is then sown, and just raked in lightly; the whole is immediately covered with brush for shelter to keep it warm, and a slight fence thrown around it.

In this condition it remains until the frosts are all gone, when the brush is taken off, and the young plants are exposed to the nutritive and genial warmth of the sun, which quickly invigorates them in an astonishing degree, and soon renders them strong and large enough to be removed for planting, especially if they be not sown too thick.

Every tobacco planter, assiduous to secure a sufficient quantity of plants, generally has several of these plant-beds in different situations, so that if one should fail another may succeed; and an experienced planter commonly takes care to have ten times as many plants as he can make use of.

In these beds along with the tobacco they generally sow kale, colewort, and cabbage-seeds, etc. at the same time.

There are seven different kinds of tobacco, particularly adapted to the different qualities of the soil on which they are cultivated, and each varying from the other. They are named Hudson, Frederick, Thick joint, Shoe-string, Thick-set, Sweet-scented, and Oroonoko.

But although these are the principal, yet there are a great many different species besides, with names peculiar to the situations, settlements, and neighbourhoods, wherein they are produced, which it would be too tedious here to specify and particularise.

The soil for tobacco must be rich and strong.

The ground is prepared in this manner; viz. after being well broke up, and by repeated working, either with the plough or handhoes, rendered soft, light, and mellow, the whole field is made into hills, each to take up the space of three feet and flattened on the top.

In the first rains, which are here called seasons, after the vernal equinox, the tobacco plants are carefully drawn while the ground is soft, carried to the field where they are to be planted, and one dropped upon every hill which is done by the negro-children; the most skilful slaves then begin planting them, by making a hole with their finger in each hill, inserting the plant with the tap-root carefully placed straight down, and pressing the earth close on each side of it. This is continued as long as the ground is wet enough to enable the plants to take root, or there be plants sufficiently grown to draw and set; and it requires several different seasons, or periods of rain, to enable them to complete planting their crop, which operation is frequently not finished until July.

After the plants have taken root, and begin to grow, the ground is carefully weeded, and worked either with hand-hoes or the plough, according as it will admit. After the plants have considerably increased in bulk, and begin to shoot up, the tops are pinched off, and only ten, twelve, or sixteen leaves left, according to the quality of the tobacco and the soil.

The worms also are carefully picked off and destroyed, of which there are two species that prey upon tobacco.

One is the ground-worm, which cuts it off just beneath the surface of the earth, this must be carefully looked for, and trodden to death. It is of a dark-brown colour, and short.

The other is the horn-worm, some inches in length, as thick as your little finger, of a vivid green colour, with a number of pointed excrescences, or feelers, from his head like horns: these devour the leaf, and are always upon the plant.

As it would be endless labour to keep their hands constantly in search of them, it would be almost impossible to prevent their eating up more than half the crop had it not been discovered that turkeys are particularly dexterous at finding them, eat them up voraciously, and prefer them to every other food. For this purpose every planter keeps a flock of turkeys, which he has driven into the tobacco grounds every day by a little negroe that can do nothing else; these keep his tobacco more clear from horn-worms, than all the hands he has got could do, were they employed solely for that end.

When the tops are nipped off, a few plants are left untouched for seed. On the plants that have been topped young sprouts are apt to spring out, which are termed suckers, and are carefully and constantly broken off lest they should draw too much of the nourishment and substance from the leaves of the plant. This operation is also performed from time to time, and is called suckering tobacco.

For some time before it is ripe, or ready for cutting, the ground is perfectly covered with the leaves which have increased to a prodigious size; and then the plants are generally about three feet high.

When it is ripe, a clammy moisture or perspiration comes forth upon the leaves which appear as it were ready to become spotted, and they are then of a great weight and substance.

When the tobacco is cut it is done when the sun is powerful, but not in the morning nor evening: the plant if large is split down the middle three or four inches, and cut off two or three inches below the extremity of the split: it is then turned directly bottom upwards, for the sun to kill it more speedily, to enable the slaves to carry it out of the field, else the leaves would break off in transporting it to the scaffolds.

The plants are cut only as they become ripe, for a whole field never ripens together. There is generally a second cutting likewise, for the stalk vegetates, and shoots forth again; and in good land with favourable seasons there is sometimes a third cutting also cured; notwithstanding acts of the legislature to prevent cutting tobacco a second time.

When the tobacco plants are cut and brought to the scaffolds, which are generally erected all round the tobacco houses, they are . . . then placed on the scaffold, with the tobacco thus suspended in the middle to dry or cure, and are called *tobacco sticks.*

As the plants advance in curing the sticks are removed from the scaffolds out of doors into the tobacco house, on other scaffolds erected therein in successive regular gradation from the bottom to the top of the roof, being placed higher as the tobacco approaches to a perfect cure, until the house is all filled, and the tobacco quite cured; and this cure is frequently promoted by making fires on the floor below.

When the tobacco house is quite full, and there is still more tobacco to bring in, all that is within the house is struck or taken down, and carefully placed in bulks, or regular rows one upon another, and the whole covered with trash tobacco, or straw, to preserve it in a proper condition, that is moist, which prevents its wasting and crumbling to pieces.

But to enable them to strike the cured tobacco they must wait for what is there called a season, that is rainy or moist weather, when the plants will then bear handling, for in dry weather the leaves would all crumble to pieces in the attempt. By this means a tobacco house may be filled two, three, or four times in one year.

Every night the negroes are sent to the tobacco house to strip, that is to pull off the leaves from the stalk, and tie them up in hands or bundles; this is also their daily occupation in rainy weather. In stripping they are careful to throw away all the ground leaves, and faulty tobacco, binding up none but what is merchantable. The hands or bundles thus tied up are also laid in what is called a bulk, and covered with the refuse tobacco or straw, to preserve their moisture.

After this the tobacco is carefully packed in hogsheads, and pressed down with a large beam laid over it, on the ends of which prodigious weights are suspended, the other end being inserted with a mortice in a tree, close to which the hogshead is placed; this vast pressure is continued for some days, and then the cask is filled up again with tobacco until it will contain no more; after which it is headed up, and carried to the public warehouses for inspection.

At these warehouses two skilful planters constantly attend, and receive a salary from the public for that purpose. They are sworn to inspect, with honesty, care, and impartiality, all the tobacco that comes to the warehouse, (and none is allowed to be shipped without being regularly inspected.)

The cask is taken off, and the tobacco is opened by means of large long iron wedges, and great labour, in such places as the inspectors direct; after this strict and attentive examination, if they find it good and merchantable, it is replaced in the cask, weighed at the public scales, the weight of the tobacco, and of the cask also, cut in the wood on the cask, stowed away in the public warehouses, and a note given to the proprietor, which he disposes of to the merchant, and neither sees nor has any trouble with his tobacco more . . .

But if the tobacco is found to be totally bad, and refused as unmerchantable, the whole is publickly burnt, in a place set apart for that purpose.*

Many problems plagued the early industry, notably that of overproduction. Planters could not be controlled. They were busy everywhere. The tobacco economy of Virginia and Maryland alternatively suffered from failure and inflation. By 1722, the prime cost of tobacco per pound had fallen to three-fourths pence a pound. In the seventeenth century, the usual method of marketing was to consign the tobacco, packed in hogsheads, to an English merchant, who sold it on commission and supplied needed manufactured goods in return. Under the system imposed by importers,

*Reprinted with the permission of Arents Collections, The New York Public Library, Astor, Lenox, and Tilden Foundations.

planters were forced to pay freight, duties, and other charges. This system proved unsatisfactory to the planter, because of both the delay involved in the transaction and the risk encountered in dealing with merchants who were often unscrupulous. In the eighteenth century, another method of marketing came into general use. The crop was sold at the farm to a local British agent, who maintained a "store" where the planter might secure the manufactured items he needed. This represented an improvement over the old system, but when the Revolution began, many planters—Thomas Jefferson among them—found themselves in the debtor class.

George Washington, a big planter, had often complained of the low prices his tobacco brought before he turned from farming to commanding troops. But during the six years of the War of Independence, tobacco helped finance the American cause. (Revolutionary soldiers themselves used tobacco to relieve stress.) "If you can't send money, send tobacco," Washington told the home front. Tobacco was sufficiently important to prompt the British armies, tramping across the Southern fields in 1780–81, to destroy thousands of hogsheads of the cured leaf in a military action that has been called the "Tobacco War." During the conflict, Jefferson expressed the hope that wheat would supplant tobacco as the staple crop of Virginia, but when peace came, the Southern planters returned with vigor to the tobacco culture.

Before the eighteenth century came to an end, the first serious antitobacco tract in America was published by a signer of the Declaration of Independence: Dr. Benjamin Rush's "Observations upon the influence of the Habitual use of Tobacco upon Health, Morals, and Property," which appeared in print in 1798 in his book *Essays,*

Literary, Moral and Philosophical. Tobacco was connected with liquor in Dr. Rush's mind, and he wrote that "One of the usual effects of smoking and chewing is thirst. This thirst cannot be allayed by water, for no sedative or even insipid liquor will be relished after the mouth and throat have been exposed to the stimulus of the smoke, or juice of Tobacco. A desire of course is excited for strong drinks, and these when taken between meals soon lead to intemperance and drunkenness." He went on to describe "one of the greatest sots" he ever knew, who acquired "a love for ardent spirits by swallowing cuds of Tobacco." This gentleman died of dropsy (under the good doctor's care) in the year 1780, according to the account. But Dr. Rush also objected to tobacco on grounds that it had disastrous effects on the stomach, the nerves, and the oral cavity. The use of tobacco, furthermore, he thought, tended to idleness, uncleanliness, and poor manners. Such warnings were to be repeated later by antismoking forces, but Rush's strictures went unheeded. Tobacco continued to imbed itself ever more deeply in the habits of Americans.

Pipe-smoking was the most common nicotian habit in early America. But snuffing had been developed into an elaborate ritual by the French, and by the first half of the eighteenth century, the snuffbox had become the mark of a gentleman in both London and Virginia. Although snuff was associated with an aristocratic way of life many Americans hated, several small snuff mills were set up in America, one of them by a French Huguenot emigré Pierre Lorillard, in New York City, on the high road to Boston at Chatham Street. The present-day P. Lorillard Co., the nation's oldest tobacco manufacturer, traces back to that beginning. Chewing, an aboriginal custom, was abhorrent to the conquerors of the New World, but gradually the habit was taken up in both Europe and America. Sailors chewed on both sides of the Atlantic.

With the nineteenth century came something new in the history of smoking: the cigar age. The pipe held its grip, as did chewing tobacco. Snuff went into eclipse. By the end of the 1800's, the cigarette would begin to make inroads. But from the time when, in New Orleans, "Spanish" cigars began to be made for domestic consumption, and especially after 1810, when Cuban cigars became a regular article of trade, stogies were the smoke of the century. At first, there was thought to be something a little too daring about the cigar, but in the main, cigar-smokers were identified with acceptably dashing, manly traits. Later, of course, cigars—large, black ones—came to be associated primarily with well-fed, cajoling, conniving politicians. The Indian peace pipe found its two-party modern American equivalent in the "smoke-filled room."

Long before the cigar became fashionable, indeed even as the Revolution was being fought along the Atlantic Coast, and earlier, pioneer settlers trickled from the Chesapeake and Carolina colonies into Kentucky and Tennessee. They followed a routine of settlement much the same as that followed by the indentured servants of tidewater days who cleared land on the piedmont. Corn and beets could be planted before the land was actually cleared, but the best virgin land was reserved for tobacco. Tobacco in the East gradually tended to become one of several money crops, although in 1803, cotton passed it as the leading U.S. export. Jefferson, the architect of Western expansion, had suggested in 1784 in his "Notes on the State of Virginia" that tobacco could serve as a useful economic prop for orderly growth; the leaf-growers of what is now the Burley region of parts of Ohio and Missouri as well as Kentucky and Tennessee can thank him yet for the Louisiana Purchase, which assured economic underpinning, including barge transportation down the Mississippi to the port of New Orleans, for them. By 1830, the Western fields were turning out a third of the nation's tobacco crop, and from 1843 until the Civil War, about half. After 1840, tobacco was grown in the Republic of Texas and traded across the Rio Grande for Mexican sugar and coffee. When 50,000 men went West during the Gold Rush, tobacco, coffee, and sugar were sold for their weight in gold dust. Competition from the Western tobacco-raisers spurred reforms in plantation methods in Maryland and Virginia, where the old "soil-mining" techniques were challenged successfully by a movement emphasizing crop rotation, diversification, and application of fertilizers.

Richmond, quite naturally, became the first tobacco manufacturing capital of the nation. The most famous of the early tobacco manufacturers was James Thomas, Jr., who got his start buying leaf for the French tobacco monopoly. In the early 1830's, Thomas started to manufacture, and when the gold fever began to sweep the country, he moved into California and won a stranglehold on the plug trade in that state. Nearly two decades later, on hearing of the firing at Fort Sumter, Thomas shipped all the tobacco he could to agents abroad and stored as much more as his facilities would hold. In the years of blockade and shortage that followed, he profited handsomely enough to equip a battery of Confederate artillery at his own expense. Earlier, another Richmonder, Robert A. Mayo, had begun to supply the U.S. Navy with plug under the name Navy Tobacco, much imitated later on. When the local Whig newspaper objected to his contractual relationship with the federal government and opposed his candidacy for public office in 1850, the reply of the Democratic newspaper became a classic of tobacco lore: "Mr. Mayo simply sells his tobacco to the United States Government and gives a *quid pro quo.*"

Tobacco factories in Virginia and North Carolina multiplied from 119 in 1840 to 348 in 1860. Richmond in that year had more than 50 factories, which employed 3,400 hands and turned out goods valued at nearly $5 million. But if Richmond, Danville, Petersburg, and Lynchburg had leaf, New York had money, salesmen, and a vast labor pool. New York's concentration of plug factories was second only to Virginia's, and, in this period, also beginning to take the play in cigar-manufacturing away from New England, where John Quincy Adams, a connoisseur of Havanas, had made the cigar respectable. To the antebellum Virginia manufacturer, the concept of salesmanship seemed remote. He expected his product to sell itself. In the Northern cities, cigars, chewing tobacco, and snuff were given a rich variety of "selling" names—The People's Choice, Daniel Webster, Cherry Ripe. As the financial capital of the nation, New York was the logical marketing center for many products, including tobacco. Most of the Virginia output went on consignment to New York factors, who in turn sold it to wholesale jobbers around the country. Many Southern retail houses actually got Virginia plug from New York distributors. The consignment system, in fact, played some part in turning South against North. During the financial panic of 1857, New York factors failed to meet their acceptances, and the burden of meeting or guaranteeing them fell on the Southern manufacturers. Seven out of eight in Richmond were reported to have suspended operations in 1857 as a direct result of defaults by their Northern agents.

All was not smooth sailing for the tobacco pushers. During the pre-Civil War period, a group of educators, clergymen, a few doctors, and the great P. T. Barnum formed an alliance to fight the tobacco habit. They were joined by a Virginian, John Hartwell Cocke, cofounder of the University of Virginia, who took part in the antislavery and anti-liquor as well as antitobacco movements. General Cocke early ceased raising the leaf himself on his land and published a sweeping denunciation under the blunt title *Tobacco, the Bane of Virginia Husbandry.* He also disseminated antitobacco tracts to adults and antitobacco medals to small boys. Some ministers made a career out of saving smokers, encouraged by such physicians as Dr. Joel Shew, who attributed insanity, impotency, perverted sexuality, and cancer to chewing. Orson S. Fowler, an authority on eugenics and phrenology, saw tobacco as essentially erotic: "No man can be virtuous as a companion who eats tobacco: for, although he may not violate the seventh commandment, yet the feverish state of the system which it produces necessarily causes a craving and lustful exercise of amativeness. . . . You, who would be pure in your love-instinct, cast this sensualizing fire from you."

Many, including in time John Quincy Adams, announced that they had shaken the habit with consequent improvement in health. Dr. R. T. Trall warned that the struggle to quit would be hard: "Ghosts and goblins, spooks and apparitions, haunt his brain; and snakes and serpents of all shapes, sizes, colors, forms and lengths dance attendance around the room, each in dumb-show chanting the praises of Tobacco. . . . All through the long night do these fiends of a disordered nervous system play their fantastic tricks to his torment; and as the morning dawns, the wretched victim of a miserable habit feels utterly prostrated." Dr. Trall reported that America had the highest per capita use of tobacco in the world, that urchins in New York from age three to six were smoking. "And more and worse than all this: Some of the *ladies* of this refined and fashion-forming metropolis are aping the silly ways of some pseudo-accomplished foreigners, in smoking Tobacco through a weaker and more feminine article,

which has been most delicately denominated cigarette."
Some antismoking literature addressed itself to youth.
The Reverend George Trask of Boston published in 1852
a tract with the engaging title *Thoughts and Stories for
American Lads; or Uncle Toby's Anti-Tobacco Advice to
his Nephew Billy Bruce.*

With the smoking custom well into its fourth century,
the *Lancet*, an English medical journal, in 1856–57 featured "The Great Tobacco Question," in which fifty
doctors expressed their views. A Dr. Hodgkin associated
tobacco with the increase of crime. A Dr. Solly associated
it with nervous paralysis and loss of intellectual capacity.
And a Dr. Schneider wrote, without documentation, that,
"so frequently is vision impaired by the constant use of
tobacco, that spectacles may be said to be part and parcel
of a German, as a hat is to an Englishman. In America,
likewise, where my practice has been extended, I have
noted the same pernicious effects, and it is a well attested
fact that the Americans wear themselves out by the use of
tobacco." But the *Lancet* itself commented editorially
that "the use of tobacco is widely spread, more widely than
any one custom, form of worship, or religious belief, and
that therefore it must have some good or at least pleasur-
able effects; that, if its evil effects were so dreadful as
stated the human race would have ceased to exist."

One of the most active reformers in the United States,
Horace Greeley, publisher of the *New York Tribune,*
whose attitude toward what he called "narcotic sensual-
ism" stemmed in part from an unfortunate experience with
a cigar at the age of six, coined, or at least popularized, the
description of the cigar as "a fire at one end and a fool at
the other." But despite his efforts and those of many more
antismoking adherents during the Gold Rush era and in
the prosperity of the early 1850's, an upturn in the use of
tobacco was observed. The fools and their fires were not
easily parted.

✦ 3

Cigarettes Come Home

CIGARETTES INCUBATED IN NEW YORK as an exotic novelty for a long time before they were accepted in the United States. How did they get to the city in the first place?

It would seem logical for the cigarette-smoking habit to have made its way north from pre-Columbian Central America, where Indians at the time of the first European explorations were already puffing on reeds filled with tobacco. Some original Americans north of the Rio Grande did, in fact, partake of this early pleasure; caves in the southwestern United States have disclosed the remains of partly consumed reed cigarettes, and trappers and traders who opened the Santa Fe trail early in the nineteenth century observed cigarette-smoking in what is now New Mexico. But the modern cigarette came to the United States via another, circuitous route.

The journey started in Seville, the world's first tobacco manufacturing center, where the Mexican reed was replaced by a paper sheath to hold shredded tobacco. Early cigarettes were a by-product of the cigar. They were made from scraps of discarded cigar butt wrapped in scraps of paper. In Spain and in the Spanish colonies of the seventeenth and eighteenth centuries, the *papelete* or *cigarillo*

was considered a beggar's smoke. By the end of the eighteenth century, Cubans had begun to use paper derived
from cotton for cigarette wrappers. Sometime after 1800,
cigarettes gradually moved to Portugal, Italy, and southern
Russia. For a while, they were seen in Japan. Then, suddenly, they showed up in France, where in 1843 the government made the cigarette part of the state tobacco
monopoly. The word "cigarette" is of French origin. But
it took its discovery by the British and the British example
of cigarette-smoking to create interest in America.

British soldiers encountered cigarettes being smoked
by Russians during the Crimean War of 1854–56. British
officers introduced them as a curiosity to their London
clubs after the war. At first, men who smoked cigarettes
on the streets of London were laughed at. But it was
cheaper to roll your own than to buy cigars. Gradually,
they caught on. Robert Gloag, a veteran of the Crimean
War, is credited with opening the first British cigarette
factory. That was in 1856. His early product bore the
enigmatic name Sweet Threes. In the late 1850's, Philip
Morris, a London tobacco merchant, went into the manufacture of cigarettes. Both Gloag and Morris cigarettes
were heavy with Latakia, a smoke-cured variety of Turkish
tobacco. About this time, Americans traveling to England
began to bring cigarettes home with them.

More sensitive to foreign influences, more faddist, perhaps, than other Americans, New Yorkers took to the
unusual fragrance of the Turkish leaf. At first, it was the
pungent flavor of the mild, aromatic Turkish leaf that
gave the cigarette its appeal. Before the Civil War, the
only cigarettes known in the United States were those that
trickled in from England and, to a lesser extent, from
Cuba. After the war, small-scale manufacturing began in
New York; hand rollers were imported from Russia and

Poland to satisfy the demand for straight Turkish cigarettes. The long, handmade American cigarettes, at first
labeled "Turkish," with "Russian" tips, were not cheap.
Sometime before 1870, a shop operated by the Bedrossian
brothers first used domestic Bright tobacco in cigarettes.
That move was observed by F. S. Kinney, an alert New
Yorker who imported European rollers to teach his factory
hands how to make cigarettes, blending the expensive
Turkish with the less expensive Bright. In that same
year, Kinney also started to produce cigarettes in Richmond.

Cigarettes appealed to a more prosperous and refined
public than chewing tobacco and pipes had reached, or
even cigars. Cigarette trademarks had a certain hauteur.
Kimball's Peerless Tobacco Works in Rochester, New
York, which produced about one-sixth of the cigarettes
consumed in the early days, advertised half a dozen brands
in 1885: Vanity Fair, Fragrant Vanity Fair, Cloth of Gold,
Three Kings, Old Gold, and Orientals. Allen & Ginter of
Richmond came up with trademarks such as Bon Ton,
Napoleons, Dubec, The Pet, and Opera Puffs. Baltimore
produced Estrella, High Life, Melrose, and Golden Age—
made by Marburg and Felgner. But for decades, the cigarette stayed far down on the totem pole in terms of consumption. The view persisted that they were too delicate
to be a man's smoke and too masculine for women.

In truth, smoking in any form was nicely attuned to the
nervous urban civilization that was beginning to dominate
American style. Tobacco supplied something romantic that
was missing. The trade sensed this. As European apothecaries had promoted the medicinal use of the mysterious
"heathen wound plant" in the 1600's, so the wholesalers
and retailers of New York in the 1870's and 1880's called
on the lore and lure of the American Indian and of the

mysterious East to sell smokes. It was good sales psychology to keep alive the link between tobacco and the noble savage. Many manufacturers and shopkeepers adorned invoice forms with a "Great Spirit" woodcut showing a mystical, nature-worshiping American Indian with his calumet outstretched to a burning volcano. This mystique was further commercialized by the wooden Indians stationed outside tobacconists' shops. (In Chicago, "Big Chief Me-Smoke-Em" became a landmark.) But the streets of New York were also populated with turbaned Turks and other glamorous wooden figures, which were mounted on wheels and rolled into the shops at closing time.

By 1880, there were three tobacco firms in Richmond making cigarettes. Allen & Ginter was one. Lewis Ginter, a New Yorker, had established himself as a merchant-importer in Richmond in the 1840's. Returning to Richmond in 1872, after serving as a major in the Confederate army, he entered into partnership with John F. Allen. Allen & Ginter began making cigarettes in 1875. The firm soon departed from the use of foreign tobacco for the new product and substituted Richmond Straight Cut No. 1. This experiment showed that Bright tobacco cigarettes had appeal. They were cheap, for one thing, and they provided a light smoke. Allen & Ginter showed great talent in packaging and salesmanship. Their cigarette displays at the Centennial celebration in Philadelphia in 1876 were so impressive that some writers thought the Philadelphia exposition marked the birth of the cigarette as well as the telephone. By 1888, the firm was producing 2 million cigarettes a day, or about 704 million a year. In that same year, the Duke firm of Durham, North Carolina, produced 744 million cigarettes—more than the national output when Duke had begun to tool up several years before.

Duke was one great name to emerge from the rubble of

the Civil War. Washington Duke, whose redheaded son James Buchanan later formed the American Tobacco Company, belonged to the independent, small-farmer class of the ante-bellum South. He had only one house servant and no field hands. As a middle-aged widower he was called into the Confederate forces and, when the Confederacy collapsed, was put for a time in Libby Prison in Richmond. He walked the 130 miles from New Bern, where he was paroled, back to his farm near Durham. With a single coin in his pocket, he surveyed his looted farm. In one of the outhouses he discovered a quantity of Bright tobacco that had somehow escaped the notice of the foraging troops. The tobacco had mellowed with age. In a small log barn, Duke had his three sons beat it, sift it, and pack it in muslin bags. They took it to town in a mule-drawn wagon and bartered it for needed provisions.

Washington Duke became convinced that Bright tobacco had a future. He set up a small factory on his farm. Then, in 1874, he shifted operations to a location in Durham near the railroad station. There he and his sons built a three-storied factory with a false front and a bell tower. As superintendent of the cigarette department, the Dukes employed one of America's pioneer cigarette-rollers, J. M. Siegel, a Russian Jew who, after learning his craft in the government factories of Kovno, emigrated first to London, then to New York, and on to Durham. Another important member of the growing labor force was Moses Gladstein, who had learned the trade in Kiev. Before joining the Dukes in Durham, Gladstein had worked with the cigarette-maker Kinney Brothers in New York City.

The Duke business grew steadily but not sensationally until 1883. Then the big break came. In that year, the Dukes leased the cigarette machine invented by James Bonsack of Virginia. The Bonsack machine had been rejected by the big-four companies on grounds that it was not reliable and people would not accept machine-made cigarettes. The Dukes swept both arguments aside. Between them, they and Bonsack's mechanic, William T. O'Brien, improved the machine. By 1884, they had it set up to make 120,000 cigarettes a day—a rate about fifty times that of hand rollers. For once, the South got the jump on New York. The cigarette girls in New York were well trained, but they could not hope to match the production of the Bonsack machine. The Dukes made another stroke for new business in 1883, when Congress voted to reduce the cigarette tax inaugurated during the Civil War. They promptly cut their prices in half. Their cigarettes became the cheapest on the market, and they sent salesmen throughout the world to peddle their box of ten cigarettes for 5 cents.

The Dukes were determined that no surplus stock of tobacco would pile up in their warehouses, and they sensed that it was important to find urban outlets. In 1884, J. B. Duke went to New York to get the feel of the growing market. There he set up a branch in a loft on Rivington Street not far from the Bowery. "Buck," as the family called him, took a cheap room, prowled the tobacco shops, talked to clerks and customers, and visited the jobbers' offices. Out of his experience, he developed a daring scheme of promotion, using, at first, picture cards of actresses, baseball players, boxers, and other notables. The acknowledged king of cigarette advertising was Major Lewis Ginter, who had won a worldwide reputation by stuffing packages with puzzles, maps, and pictures of boats, flags, actors, and actresses in numbered sets. Allen & Ginter also distributed a booklet showing famous buildings, ranging from the Egyptian Temple of Kom Omboo to the state capitols. But Duke was able to steal some of the play with a folding album of "Sporting Girls." He also sent a polo team on roller skates across the country to advertise his Cross Cut Polo Team cigarettes and smoking tobacco. In 1886, making his first open bid for the then minuscule feminine market, Duke introduced the Cameo brand in New York. The few daring women who tried it pronounced it "a perfect scream."

Edward Featherston Small, an aggressive Duke salesman, did much to build the family fortunes. Finding Atlanta unmoved by his goods, for example, he threw out the established Indian motif and scattered the city with pictures of Madame Rhea, a popular French actress, with her arm on a pedestal supporting a box of Duke cigarettes. In St. Louis, when retailers ignored him, Small advertised for a saleswoman. A petite, thin-lipped widow, a Mrs. Leonard, applied for the job and was accepted. This little stunt gave the Dukes thousands of dollars of free publicity in the local newspapers. Although he left the Duke firm to join Allen & Ginter and left the cigarette business altogether when those two firms were combined to form the American Tobacco Company, Small clung to the conviction that he had made more cigarette customers than any other man.

Duke advertising was direct and to the point. It even boasted of the Bonsack machine. A label on its Pin Head brand read: "These cigarettes are manufactured on the Bonsack Cigarette Machine." Duke wanted to beat the big manufacturers at their own game. The firm plowed much of its profits into advertising; in 1889, it put the staggering sum of $800,000 into promotion. The cigarette industry was not a major factor in newspaper and periodical advertising in the 1880's, however. Tobacco lineage did not even approach that bought to sell soaps and baking powders. Premiums, rebates, and bribes characterized the early selling of the cigarette, and, as if resources weren't already sufficiently strained, the manufacturers about this time also began to engage in price wars.

It was not clear at first that a new smoking pattern was establishing itself. Cigarettes were regarded as a fad that might go away. Growing acceptance was accompanied by waves of opposition, and during the period 1897–1901 consumption actually declined. J. B. Duke later admitted that he became afraid the cigarette business would be destroyed. He moved to diversify by purchasing several establishments manufacturing small-sized cigars and also obtained for the American Tobacco Company a larger share of the nation's plug business. But cigarette consumption began to climb upward again. Elderly housewives in the woods of Maine or the remote regions of the Far West were known to take a puff now and again, just as their mothers and grandmothers had occasionally smoked clay pipes. Some Bohemian ladies flourished specially made little cigars, and a few maidens puffed cigarettes while waiting their turn at croquet. But use was largely restricted to adult males.

Meanwhile, a fierce trade war developed, and Duke began to acquire other companies. This was in the era when the Rockefeller oil and other giant trusts were being formed. The leading tobacco firms decided that if they couldn't beat Duke they might as well join him. Allen & Ginter held out for a while, but in 1890 the five leading firms combined into the American Tobacco Company. J. B. Duke, who had just celebrated his thirty-third birthday, was elected president. The new combine controlled about nine-tenths of the nation's cigarette manufacture. It purchased exclusive use of the Bonsack machine and profited immediately from centralized management and lack of competition.

Among the first to attack the tobacco combine were a group of farmers in western Kentucky and Tennessee. In 1904, they formed a "protective association" for the dark tobacco grown in the Black Patch area. When independent local planters, called the "Hill Billies," continued to deal with the trust, the association struck back. Masked "Night Riders" stormed a town in Kentucky and wrecked tobacco factories. Finally, after a series of incidents including destruction of plant-beds and harvested crops, and whippings and murders, government troops were called into Black Patch country to restore order. A few years later, the tobacco combine was attacked by the federal government under the Sherman Antitrust Act, and, following a 1911 Supreme Court decision, the trust was broken up. Four firms emerged—American, Reynolds, Liggett & Myers, and Lorillard. Renewed competition increased the cost of selling and advertising, which jumped from $18.1 million in 1910 to $32.4 million in 1913.

During the quarter century between the surrender at Appomattox and the formation of the American Tobacco Company, the antiliquor forces continued, as an extracurricular activity, to snipe at tobacco in all forms. A reformed drunkard and temperance lecturer, John B. Gough, would pull from his pocket a square of tobacco, smell it as if it were a rose, cry out, "Ah, you black devil, I love you," and throw it away. In 1868, James Parton, the biographer, delivered his sentiments on smoking and drinking in three essays. Parton said, among other things, that women counted tobacco a rival in men's affections. To this "impertinent falsehood." the *Overland Monthly*, Bret Harte's journal, commented: "Shocking as it may seem to Mr. Parton, the young Prince of the maiden's vision generally comes to her dreams driving a fast horse and smoking a cigar." To prove the point, the journal cited evidence of

nicotine in Charlotte Brontë's *Jane Eyre* and *Villette.*
Waves were made in 1880 when the General Conference
of the Methodist Episcopal Church resolved that preach-
ers seeking admission to the conference were expected to
answer in the affirmative the question: "Will you wholly
abstain from the use of tobacco?" The Methodists had
been divided, along Northern and Southern lines, on the
tobacco question during the Reconstruction Period. But
the Southerners gradually moved nearer the Northern
position.

Men who turned to cigarette-smoking were denounced
as effeminate. "The decadence of Spain began when the
Spaniards adopted cigarettes," the *New York Times*
warned editorially on January 29, 1884, "and if this
pernicious practice obtains among adult Americans the
ruin of the republic is close at hand." Women who puffed
on the little white roll were considered loose; moralists of
the 1860's held that "when one hears of sly cigarettes between feminine lips at croquet parties, there is no more
to be said!" Women were warned that they would become
sterile, grow a masculine mustache, come down with tuberculosis. "Cigarette girls" of several eras became, like Carmen, archetypes of recklessness and sin. In Kansas, a
traveling Chautauqua company staging scenes from Bizet's
opera presented a cast against a backdrop showing a dairy
rather than a cigarette factory, and Carmen herself walked
on stage carrying a milk pail. Such was the climate of
opinion in rural areas, where the anticigarette movement
was especially strong.

The greatest warrior in the anticigarette campaign was
Lucy Page Gaston, a Midwesterner who trained on the
official Women's Christian Temperance Union publication and then moved over into the antitobacco movement
in the 1890's. She led a Chicago-based campaign modeled

on the antialcohol campaign. Children were mobilized to wear pins, sing songs, carry banners, parade, and preach sermons to their elders. They jeered at smoking with the belligerency of the righteous young and threw a panic into the industry. Clergymen, educators, and many businessmen applauded Miss Gaston's efforts. Among the religious groups, the Society of Friends and the Methodists took the strongest stand. At a general conference of 1900 in Chautauqua, tobacco was censured, although some of the Quakers expressed concern lest tea-drinking also become a vice in the eyes of their fellows. Cigar-makers publicly decried the anticigarette attacks but privately organized their own whispering campaigns. Rumors flew that cigarette paper had been bleached with arsenic. Tobacco used in cigarettes was also downgraded. It was said that much of it came from derelicts paid to retrieve cigar butts from the streets and gutters. Boxing champion John L. Sullivan denounced cigarettes as unmanly. Henry Ford and the popular writer Elbert Hubbard spoke against the cigarette. Thomas Edison refused to hire cigarette-smokers. A nationwide "Committee to Study the Tobacco Problem" was established and attracted distinguished men in every field, philanthropist George Foster Peabody among them.

Anticigarette physicians included Sir William Osler, Surgeon General Rupert Blue, Walter B. Cannon of Harvard, and Harvey W. Wiley (father of the Pure Food and Drug Act of 1906). These men agreed in condemning cigarettes, but they disagreed on their reasons. In 1912, a Dr. Tidswell opined that "the most common cause of female sterility is the abuse of tobacco by males . . . those countries which use most tobacco have the largest number of stillbirths." Early crusaders coined the term "nicotinic amblyopia" to name "a peculiar weakening of sight brought on by smoking." Lacking laboratory evidence, they nevertheless made allegations that "coffin nails" caused moral delinquency, mental deficiency, and many grave maladies. Tuberculosis and pneumonia were widely mentioned. Boys were warned that "with every breath of cigarette smoke you inhale imbecility and exhale manhood." And not only would smoking reduce virility but smokers also were headed for an early grave. One early antitobacco crusader, Charles M. Fillmore, who linked smoking with longevity, foreshadowed the statistical alarm of the 1950's when he said: "The New England Life Insurance Company found, after investigating records of 180,-000 policyholders, that during a certain period 57 out of 100 nonusers of tobacco died; during the same period, 95 out of 100 cigarette smokers died."

Free cures were offered in many cities. Antismoking clinics offered a program for penitent sufferers consisting of a wholesome diet, a mouthwash of silver nitrate solution, and gentian root to chew as a substitute for a smoke. In search of a story, some reporters in Chicago posed as cigarette victims and went through a clinic cure. They reported that they became deathly sick when they returned to their cigarettes. Patent medicines to help smokers break the habit were also put on the market. One of the most widely advertised was No-to-bac; its slogan was "Don't tobacco-spit your life away."

Muckraker Upton Sinclair found the scene amusing. In his book on the Chicago meat-packing industry, *The Jungle,* he wrote: "It was quite touching, the zeal of people to see that his health and happiness were provided for. Did the person wish to smoke? There was a little discourse about cigars, showing him exactly why the Thomas Jefferson Five-cent Perfecto was the only cigar worthy of the name. Had he, on the other hand, smoked too much? Here was a remedy for the smoking habit, twenty-five doses for a quarter and a cure absolutely guaranteed in ten doses."

Antismoking legislation was passed. First, in New York, it was made a misdemeanor for any person "actually or apparently under 16 years of age" to smoke in public. Then a federal statute in 1897 prohibited the use of coupons and other extraneous articles in cigarette packages. Tennessee courts held that cigarettes were not legitimate articles of commerce. In 1901, New Hampshire made it illegal for any person, firm, or corporation to make, sell, or keep for sale any form of cigarette. Under an Illinois statute, enacted on June 3, 1907, the manufacture, sale, or gift of a cigarette "containing any substance deleterious to health, including tobacco" was made punishable by a fine of not more than $100 or imprisonment in county jail for not more than thirty days. By 1909, twelve states and numerous towns and cities had enacted restrictive laws of one sort or another. The state laws were directed solely against cigarettes—not pipes or cigars. Even in New York, where the cigarette enjoyed its first vogue, women were forbidden to smoke in public. A survey conducted by the *Chicago Tribune* showed that only Wyoming and Louisiana had failed to pass any antismoking legislation.

It is difficult to know for sure how this legislation affected cigarette sales. In 1909, when the last of the state laws was passed, national sales were twice what they had been five years before. Cigarettes had won general public acceptance. But as insurance the big tobacco companies took steps toward diversification before and after World War I.

During that war, cigarette consumption increased still further. Echoing George Washington in an earlier conflict, General John J. Pershing cabled Washington, D.C.: "Tobacco is as indispensable as the daily ration; we must have thousands of tons of it without delay." Indeed, during

World War I, it looked as if the enemies of nicotine had been crushed in the stampede to send cigarettes to the boys overseas. All the nation seemed to be singing "While you've a lucifer to light your fag." But the moralists were still at it. Dr. Clarence True Wilson, head of the Methodist Temperance and Moral Board, charged that the "tobacco trust" had played on American patriotism to put dope in cigarettes so that the doughboys would become addicted. There was intolerance on the other side, too. Champions of the cigarette wondered aloud if the Espionage Act of 1917 was broad enough to cover reformers and ministers who attacked smoking.

The figures for cigarette consumption from 1913 to 1929 do not suggest controversy. The curve is upward and smooth. But once the Eighteenth Amendment to the Constitution was voted, prohibitionists revived the antitobacco movement. Billy Sunday himself declared: "Prohibition is won; now for tobacco." In 1920, the redoubtable Lucy Page Gaston announced that she would run for President on the no-tobacco issue. Some men, annoyed at feminist pretensions in general, affected horror at the idea of public puffing by their women, and went along with Miss Gaston. Others, annoyed at the rising tide of "sticky-beaking," formed smokers' leagues to defend the right to light up. Miss Gaston did not run for President, although she and other reformers continued to campaign.

Meanwhile, as the women of America began to take to smoking in large numbers, the brazen flapper became the symbolic target of opposition. A student, Alice Tanton, was expelled from Michigan State Normal College in 1922 for smoking cigarettes. The dean of women, Bessie Leach Priddy, said she had no choice but to send Miss Tanton home. An investigation showed that the coed was addicted to cigarettes before coming to Ypsilanti, the dean claimed, telling Alice, "You have had repeated warnings. But you have continued to smoke—even on the public streets. You will not be permitted to register for the spring term." In 1922, the term "student militant" was unknown. But Alice Tanton proved militant. She brought suit against college president Charles McKenney on the ground that her personal freedom had been violated. To no avail. On March 5, 1924, the Michigan Supreme Court upheld expulsion of the coed.

Successors to the antismoking leader Miss Gaston delved also into the realm of medicine. Tobacco was called a poison by some. But a few medical men, newly aware of the psychological aspects of medicine, came to the defense of tobacco—in moderation. Thereupon, the ever alert American Tobacco Company added to its Lucky Strike advertisement: "Be moderate—be moderate in all things, even in smoking." Gradually, the clamor faded. One by one, the states relaxed or dropped their antismoking statutes, some of which had never been enforced. By 1927, the legislatures had repealed all the statutes, and the anticigarette movement was legally as well as practically dead. Spurred by increased advertising, the political emancipation of women, and the widespread use of liquor during Prohibition, the tide had turned in favor of smoking.

The dynamics of taxation played a part in the acceptance of cigarettes. The first federal excise tax on cigarettes had been imposed during the Civil War to raise money for the Union war effort. These taxes were increased and then, after the war, lowered. Foes of the cigarette pressed for higher taxes. By 1919, the federal rate had jumped to 6 cents a pack. State taxes were first imposed in 1921. Some lawmakers, both state and federal, favored taxation because they considered it to be a restrictive measure. Experience showed, however, that smokers, though they might grumble, would pay whatever taxes were assessed. By the time this acquiescence was generally conceded, the fast growth of revenue to states and federal government had raised cigarette taxes to a place of importance in government budgets.

As the opposition to cigarettes died down during the 1930's, special smoking rooms were provided in theaters, railroads, and steamships, and the student government at Smith College voted to permit smoking on campus. (Subsequently, when a dormitory burned down, the smoking in Smithies' rooms was barred.) President William Allan Neilson won the hearts of the girls at Northampton when he said, in words that nicely summed up the American ambivalence on cigarette-smoking: "It is a dirty, expensive, and unhygienic habit—to which I am devoted."

4

The Ad Man:
Tobacco Road to Madison Avenue

LOOKING BACK OVER his long career, George Washington Hill, the rough impresario who wore his hat indoors and created a marketing legend with his sales campaigns, once said that he decided in about 1907 that the future of the tobacco business belonged to the cigarette. Advertising had been stepped up following dissolution of the tobacco trust in 1911, and prior to World War I, national advertising campaigns were launched for the first time to broaden the consumer base for cigarettes and boost individual consumption. But manufacturers were still spreading their promotional efforts over several brands by giving premiums and using other similar sales techniques.

Cigarette-smokers also still preferred the exotic Near Eastern blends. Fatima, a Liggett & Myers product, was the first popular brand to be marketed in the modern cup package of twenty cigarettes. It sold for 15 cents a pack. American introduced Omar, a competing Turkish blend, and Lorillard developed Zubelda. Even the straight domestic brands were seasoned with a sprinkling of Turkish. Marcus Felder, sometimes called the "father of the American cigarette," added a little Turkish tobacco to the native leaf in the storied Sweet Caporals, originally made for F. S. Kinney and later for American Tobacco, and smoked by all the young swains on the front porches of an innocent America.

But while Turkish cigarettes were gaining headway in the city, competition among manufacturers had already increased. Some of them brought out cigarette makes under the brand marks of their most popular smoking tobaccos. J. B. Duke advertised his Dukes Mixture not only for pipes but for cigarettes as well. R. J. Reynolds used a Burley blend for his Prince Albert smoking tobacco, laying the foundation for his famous Camel cigarette six years later.

It was something of a paradox that Reynolds, a staunch defender of Bright, should revolutionize the cigarette field with the introdutcion in 1913 of Camels, a Burley blend. Richard Joshua Reynolds was a boy of fifteen when Lee surrendered at Appomattox. He became a tobacco-peddler and in 1875 set up a plant in Winston, North Carolina, which had become a thriving manufacturing center for Bright as Danville and Lynchburg, Virginia, shrank in significance. As a manufacturer, Reynolds quickly got the hang of mass production, but the R. J. Reynolds Tobacco Company had never manufactured cigarettes prior to the formation of the trust. Dissolution found it having to start from scratch in this field. Following the Supreme Court decision breaking up the combine, Reynolds told his friend Josephus Daniels, "Watch me and see if I don't give Buck Duke hell." This he was never able to do, for the reason that Duke moved out of the tobacco business into textiles, aluminum, and other enterprises. But Reynolds did launch several cigarette brands, including Camel, the first modern cigarette.

Later, Reynolds, too, diversified into aluminum and additional products.

The Camel blend was something new. It was largely flue-cured Bright with a Turkish seasoning and a cased or sweetened Burley, its most distinctive feature. The Burley had been prepared somewhat as if it were being readied for plug tobacco. Burley had never been used in just this way in a cigarette blend. Later, in about 1916, a certain amount of Maryland leaf was added for its slow-burning qualities.

At first, Reynolds didn't realize what he had in Camels and continued to push his Reyno brand, as well as Osman, a new blend of flue-cured and Turkish. The first real sales campaign for Camels was launched in Cleveland, Ohio, where pictures and coupons and other sales gimmicks were dispensed with as an excuse to price Camels at the low rate of 10 cents for a pack of twenty cigarettes. When the trials proved successful, Reynolds decided to concentrate on one brand and push it hard. It was easier for Reynolds than the other firms that already had heavy investments in their established cigarette brands to do such a thing. All the Reynolds brands were new. In its national campaign of 1914, Reynolds adopted "teaser" advertisements, such as "Camels! Tomorrow there will be more Camels in this town than in all Asia and Africa combined!" Then came the picture on the package, clearly a concession to the early taste for Turkish leaf. Its brand image and package design were inspired by "Old Joe," a Barnum & Bailey dromedary. Reynolds spent nearly $1.5 million on advertising Camels during the brand's springboard year, and sales began to climb steadily.

When World War I cut off Turkish imports, smokers turned to the domestic brands. This switch hit Lorillard hard, since it owned the major brands of Turkish, but

Reynolds enjoyed a bit of good luck. During the war, government contracts among cigarette-makers were awarded on the basis of domestic sales, and, since Camel had from 30 to 40 per cent of the market at the outbreak of the war, Reynolds benefited. Camel became a favorite brand among the boys in France, which helped Reynolds keep its lead for a decade after the war. By the time of his death in 1918, R. J. Reynolds had 40 per cent of the nation's cigarette business.

Other manufacturers thought Camels a joke at first. But when Camel swept other brands aside, the captains of the tobacco industry revised their opinion and began a desperate search for ways to compete. Industry chemists found that the most distinctive feature of the Camel blend was the dipped Burley. That was one evident factor in its success. Another was concentration on one-brand advertising. At American Tobacco, President Percival S. Hill and his son George looked over the company's brands and picked out Lucky Strike (a name used for plug during the Gold Rush) as a likely competitor for Camels. A new package was designed, with its famous bull's-eye in the center, and a sales campaign devised around the slogan "Lucky Strike, It's Toasted." That idea came to the elder Hill when a vice president in charge of manufacturing remarked that the amount of heat used in making cigarettes was equivalent to cooking. Lucky's first advertising campaign shows a piece of toast with a fork stuck through it. This was the start of one of the most expensive, if not *the* most expensive, sales campaigns in merchandising history.

In the heat of competition, Liggett & Myers updated both the advertising and the content of its Chesterfield brand, which had been on the market since 1912. The blend eventually moved closer to the Camel formula although it had somewhat less extraneous flavoring. In

1915, Chesterfields, which had previously been sold in a slide-and-shell box, appeared in a tight paper-and-foil wrap like that used for Camels and Lucky Strikes. By 1917, there were three standard brands of cigarettes. "I'd Walk a Mile for a Camel" became the signature for Camels. Liggett & Myers came up with the slogan "They Satisfy."

By the 1920's, tobacco manufacturing had completed its long transition from a leisurely country craft to a competitive war waged on a national battlefield. In this war, advertising loomed as the heavy artillery. But the big cigarette brands had their infantry, too—the foot-slogging sales forces that carried the competitive fight all the way to the smallest retail unit. Their job was not taking orders but reinforcing the advertising for their brands. This they did in several ways: by placing display materials at or near the retail counters; by helping retailer and wholesaler rotate tobacco stocks properly; and by "maintaining distribution," that is, inducing the storekeeper to carry their brands. Their activity grew more competitive as the number of retail outlets multiplied. The tobacco salesman's stock in trade was not reliance on premiums but massive volume and rapid turnover backed up by a bombardment of advertising.

There was a certain amount of polite, conservative advertising, in the tradition long since established by the sons of Pierre Lorillard, Peter and George, who, in 1787, had started the earliest known newspaper tobacco-advertising campaign. But cigarette advertising in the 1920's was repetitious, strident—advertising "gone mad." Agencies of major cigarette accounts became scenes of frenetic energy, and advertising appeals to the consumer were largely emotional. As the growth curve of women smokers continued to rise, advertising slogans were increasingly aimed at lady customers. Youth, too, was a natural target.

Every year, millions of young people reached adolescence, a time when an interest in smoking might easily be generated. Color ads showing celebrities invitingly holding a particular brand promised social approbation to youth. Advertising that made cigarette-smoking seem like good sense, and even healthful, spurred more sales as medical doctors, athletes, and movie stars, tempted by large fees, gladly signed testimonials implying that their health and good looks (in the case of doctors, that of their patients) were in no way endangered by smoking.

The tobacco industry, during the 1920's, undertook some "educational" programs, such as National Tobacco Week, with exhibitions showing processes, as well as charts indicating the place of tobacco in the national economic life. But the advertising of individual companies did not adhere to this moderate line. While decrying the attacks of the zealous antitobacconists, Dr. James A. Tobey, in *Scribner's Magazine,* nevertheless declared them "no more unreasonable and bigoted than are some of the predatory, mercenary, and rapacious commercial tobacco interests, whose sales methods and advertising ethics, or lack of them, are, to put it mildly, definitely malodorous." Senator Reed Smoot (R., Utah) decried the "orgy of buncombe, quackery, and downright falsehood and fraud." Church and other reform groups followed this theme, criticizing specifically what they called the appeal being made to convert the youth and the women of the land to the tobacco habit. In the *Christian Century* of December 18, 1920, William K. Anderson commented on the "blatant and disgraceful advertising methods of cigarette companies in recent months," and then turned to the subject of women in the cigarette ads: "First the woman appears in the advertisement—merely a pretty girl who becomes part of the picture; then she is offering the man a fag; next she asks him to blow the smoke her way; finally she lights hers by his. The one encouraging thing about this development is that the grade of women pictured in the posters has distinctly deteriorated in the process, until now we see at the turn of the road the most voluptuous, greasy-haired Medusa that was ever used to advertise anything."

In extravagant claims, American advertisers outshone those of any other country, although cigarette consumption in some other countries, where prices were higher and consumer income lower, was greater than that in the United States. For example, Greece in 1920 had one-and-a-half times the cigarette consumption of the United States. But such facts did not deter the American manufacturers. Their noisy campaigns went blithely on. The millions spent on advertising were directed at increasing brand consciousness, capturing new smokers, and inducing shifts of allegiance. Brand loyalty was regarded as an elastic and uncertain quality that could be affected by ceaseless, importunate advertising. These programs undoubtedly resulted in experimental interest in untried brands and an increase in impulse buying. The effects of widespread publicity became the subject of study by psychologists, sociologists, economists, and others. Elaborate analyses were made of such questions as the collective phenomenon of consumer demand, consumer responsiveness to various phases of promotions, the reasons for seasonal variations in consumption, reaction to price changes, and instability of consumer preferences.

It was against this background that George Washington Hill took over American Tobacco in 1925, the year of his father's death. By then, he had acquired mastery of all phases of the tobacco business—including advertising. Even as a youth, he had trained in both the market and factory. When he left Williams College in 1904, he went to Wilson, North Carolina, to hustle in the leaf market. From the warehouse floor, where tobacco was purchased, the young Hill followed the leaf over the flue-cured belt. Then, in Durham, he ran the top floor of a stemmery. His next step was to supervise production of Carolina Bright cigarettes at the Wells-Whitehead Tobacco Company in Wilson. From there, he went on the road selling cigarettes. In 1907, he was given management of Butler-Butler, Inc., a subsidiary of American, which produced various tobacco products. Hill decided to concentrate on one product, Pall Mall, then a Turkish blend not to be confused with the domestic-blend cigarette made under the same name since 1937. The "gorgeous" red package, as Hill described it, was featured in advertising, and Hill introduced the use of magazine back-covers for advantageous display. Pall Mall became the number one bestseller among the high-grade cigarettes. Hill also pushed Egyptian Straights with the device of a gift in every package. The prize, a little silk flag, appealed to women, who collected them from their men friends to piece out pillows for their horsehair sofas. (Rival makers launched similar programs. Reviving the practice of giving coupons and premiums, some handed out Yale pennants.)

Hill displayed an ability to identify with the mores of average men and women. His ads were aggressive and occasionally in poor taste. They have even been called vulgar. Hill's competitors often felt that he hit below the belt, as when he wrote of the "sheep dip" in those cigarettes not possessing the virtues of the Lucky Strike toasting process. The Lucky Strike curing process, identical with that commonly practiced in the industry, was advertised as if it were a specialty of American Tobacco. In an open bid to crack the feminine market, Lucky Strike featured testimonials from Madame Schumann-Heink, the noted opera singer, believed to be the first woman to provide a public testimonial for a cigarette (but when a number of colleges in the West canceled her engagements, she not only refrained from praising cigarettes, she even denounced the use of tobacco). Some inhabitants of Winston-Salem, home of Camels, said that American Tobacco's Lucky Strike salesmen had initiated a whispering campaign against Camels. But it was hard to know. No commodity seemed to thrive as much on rumor as cigarettes. One time-worn story had it that lepers could be found in such-and-such a factory. It was also rumored that a certain combination of numbers on a cigarette package would win a new car from the manufacturer.

The Reynolds firm, to meet Hill's competition, changed its ad agency and hired William Cole Esty, who had earned the distinction of coining such phrases as "Undie Odor" when handling the Lux soap account. Esty moved against American Tobacco by making an indirect slap at the Lucky Strike toasting process with the slogan "It's Fun To Be Fooled." Hill, in turn, worked out a new advertising campaign for Lucky Strike with his ad agency, Lord & Thomas, whose president at the time was Albert D. Lasker. Hill apparently thought the slogan "It's Toasted" was losing its punch. A second slogan, "No Throat Irritation—No Cough," had been eclipsed by the Old Gold slogan "Not a Cough in a Carload." Old Gold was a latecomer to the battle of the brands. Its "Blindfold Test" involved printed ads featuring John Held's flappers, Petty girls, Ripley's "Believe It or Not," comic strips, and prize contests. Using every medium at its disposal, the brand fought its way into the market. But it was not in the running with the Big Three.

The Lucky Strike people's search for a new slogan ended in "Reach for a Lucky Instead of a Sweet." This slogan, which is credited with making smoking acceptable to women, was the inspiration of George Washington Hill himself. Aware that women shunned the "vice" of tobacco only because they considered it less than ladylike, Hill had been determined to change their minds almost from the moment he succeeded his father as president of American Tobacco. He wanted to tell them, through advertising, that smoking was good for their image. He chose radio as the medium for his message.

In *The Story of Tobacco in America* by Joseph C. Robert (Chapel Hill: University of North Carolina Press, 1967), Hill is quoted as recalling how the idea on which to base his first big radio campaign came to him. The passage tells much about the times and about Hill himself.

> I was riding out to my home. I got to 110th Street and Fifth Avenue; I was sitting in the car and I looked at the corner, and there was a great big stout negro lady chewing on gum. And, there was a taxicab—it was in the summertime—coming the other way. I thought, I was human and I looked, and there was a young lady sitting in the taxicab with a long cigarette holder in her mouth, and her skirts were pretty high, and she had a very good figure. I didn't know what she was smoking; maybe she was smoking a Camel.
>
> But, right then and there it hit me; there was the colored lady that was stout and chewing, and there was the young girl that was slim and smoking a cigarette—"Reach for a Lucky Instead of a Sweet."
>
> There it was, right in front of you. That campaign really went to town, as everybody knows.

It was a swell slogan, easy to say, and it tempted the sweet-eating American public to think of cigarettes every time it opened its mouth. Figure-conscious women began to respond by the thousands. An alluring series of ads was prepared to point out how much healthier it was to smoke Lucky Strikes than to eat sweets. Actress Helen Hayes gave it as her theory, in one ad, that Luckies accounted for the trim figure of modern woman. Musical comedy stars contributed evidence to support the theory, and the original Lucky poster girl, Rosalie Adele Nelson, announced that she considered herself indeed a "Lucky Girl" to have found this pleasant way to all-round health.

But as soon as the campaign began to hit its stride, the National Confectioners' Association struck a sour note by forwarding a protest to American Tobacco. The company replied evasively that it intended no slur on the candy trade (and, in fact, the battle cry may have developed first against the Lydia E. Pinkham slogan of 1891, "Reach for a Vegetable Instead of a Sweet"). A sort of guerrilla warfare began. One candy-manufacturer hired time on radio and started to say nasty things about cigarettes and their effect on the human constitution. A chain of New York candy stories inserted this paragraph in its advertising: "Do not let anyone tell you that a cigarette can take the place of a piece of candy. The cigarette will inflame your tonsils, poison with nicotine every organ of your body, and dry up your blood—nails in your coffin."

As the sniping of the candy-makers began to develop volume, letters poured in to American Tobacco and the company began to hedge a little. It inserted the word "fattening" before the word "sweets" in its advertising copy. George M. Cohan was quoted as author of the statement: "Lucky is a marvelous pal—the toasted flavor overcomes a craving for foods which add weight." But this didn't satisfy the candy-makers, either. Another concession then crept into Lucky ads. "A reasonable proportion of sugar in the diet is recommended, but the authorities are overwhelming that too many fattening sweets are harmful and that too many such are eaten by the American people," the new copy read. "So for moderation's sake we say: Reach for a Lucky Instead of a Sweet."

The fight was in dead earnest by this time. Officials representing some two dozen manufacturers and trade associations met to discuss ways and means of quashing the "fattening sweet" menace. A National Food Products Protective Committee was formed, and it was decided to launch a cooperative advertising campaign. An appeal was made to the Federal Radio Commission, predecessor of the Federal Communications Commission, to put a stop to the "unfair propaganda" that, it was alleged, was being sent to innocent thousands of listeners through the Lucky Strike radio hour. The National Confectioners' Association had already swung its guns into position. "Don't neglect your candy ration!" screamed one ad. "Read how candy saves wear and tear on body tissues—how candy can help you to your proper weight!" This was about as ingenious a way of admitting that candy is fattening as anyone could devise. A Dr. Herman Bundesen prepared a booklet setting forth the importance of candy as a food. Everyone was urged to send in for that instructive little booklet. But George Washington Hill was not ready to give in. He issued a manifesto declaring that he did not intend to give up his slogan and sent a book on rational dietetics, by another doctor, to tobacco jobbers. *Printers' Ink*, the organ of the advertising business, picked up some characteristic statements from the booklet's pages: "Sugar is undermining the nation's health. By this I mean cane sugar, beet sugar and, to a much less degree, maple sugar. The average American consumes daily a quarter pound of cane sugar . . . Sugar is very bad for children . . . It not only destroys a child's appetite, but takes the place of essential food elements in the diet. . . . Pastries and puddings are in general detrimental to health."

The tobacco-candy fight was a tough one, in which the Federal Trade Commission (FTC) became deeply enmeshed. American Tobacco appropriated $12.3 million to carry on the battle. Hill modified the slogan to "Reach for a Lucky Instead," and ran a "future-shadow" series of advertisements featuring double-chinned and heavy-belted silhouettes behind normal figures. But finally the abbreviated version of the slogan had to go, too, as the FTC banned American from selling cigarettes as a reducing device, even by implication. One interested bystander, Lorillard, cashed in with its own slogan: "Eat a Chocolate, Light an Old Gold. And Enjoy Both! Two Fine and Healthful Treats!"

Not every one of Hill's advertising campaigns was successful. Some went wrong and had to be scrapped. Others were quietly eased out by more conservative subordinates who spent most of their time trying to shield Hill from his own schemes. But by 1931, Lucky Strikes led all cigarettes in sales and alternated with Camels for the number-one spot in brand preference between 1930 and 1950.

Hill not only pushed Lucky Strikes to a position of dominance but got more out of his advertising dollar than competitors. Many broadcasters regard him as the man who really put commercial punch into broadcasting. His career in radio included sponsorship of the Metropolitan Opera, "Hit Parade," Ben Bernie, Kay Kyser, Eddy Duchin, Jack Benny, Wayne King, "Information Please," and columnist Dorothy Thompson. Among his trademarks, three stood out. Hill paid two tobacco auctioneers $25,000 each a year to sound their incomprehensible nasal chants climaxed by the clear and triumphant "S-o-o-o-old

American!" Another was the slogan "Lucky Strike Green Has Gone to War," which emerged after the gold-and-green dyes used in the paper for Lucky packages had to be discarded because components used in them were scarce and crucial to military production during World War II. The third was the dramatically enunciated "L.S./M.F.T." (Lucky Strike Means Fine Tobacco), which Hill dreamed up in 1942.

Gradually, in the two decades before Pearl Harbor, the industry and its promotional gimmicks underwent important changes. First, there was the introduction of new brand names. Old Gold had already joined the Big Three brands when, in 1933, another brand, whose name dated back to Philip Morris, the London tobacconist of the 1850's, was introduced. In the midst of the Depression, Philip Morris faced strong competition. The hiring of a diminutive page boy from the Hotel New Yorker put Philip Morris on the map. Johnny's high-pitched "Call for Philip Morris!" became one of the most familiar sounds on radio. By 1940, the brand had won 7 per cent of the national cigarette market. Brown & Williamson, originally a small snuff firm in Winston-Salem, which had been bought in 1927 by British-American Tobacco, had always held out against the one-big-brand idea. It offered specialty brands—experimenting with cork tips, filters, menthol, and the like. Appropriately, its first cigarette was named Sir Walter Raleigh. Wings and Avalon became popular low-priced brands, and B & W revived coupons with a repackaged Raleigh and with the mentholated Kool and the filter-tipped Viceroy.

In 1939, the old master George Washington Hill broke away from the one-big-brand idea and launched Pall Mall as a king-sized cigarette, 85 millimeters in length compared to "regular" 70-millimeter cigarettes. The "modern design" king-sized cigarette marked an important development, and the brand battlefield extended as kings became big factors—Herbert Tareyton, 85-millimeter Chesterfields, and so forth.

Hill ruled American Tobacco with an iron hand until his death in 1946. In the process, his reputation for ruthlessness gained the status of revealed truth among his critics. This popular image of him is rejected by some of his associates. Niles Trammell, retired third president of the National Broadcasting Company, a man who remembers him well, subscribes to the notion that Hill was the single dominant figure in the development of cigarette advertising and, by extension, of radio advertising. But Trammell says that what writers have done to Hill is cruel: "Old Hill was just interested in one thing—selling Lucky Strike cigarettes."

Whatever the truth may be, there is no argument but that Hill's slogans were the aural symbol of an era, much as Franklin Delano Roosevelt's cigarette in a long, slim holder was, for the nation and the world, one of its most striking visual symbols.

♦ 5

Cancer by the Carton?

WAS HAMLET'S FATHER done in by the "juice of cursed hebenon"? So it is claimed in one of several nineteenth-century commentaries on nicotine as an agent of murder. Literature is ornamented with countless tales of untimely deaths attributed to tobacco. Napoleon was said to have died from excessive snuffing. John Hancock, too much a gentleman to spit just anywhere, allegedly died from a series of ailments induced by swallowing tobacco juice.

From the time tobacco was first introduced to Europeans, it attracted strong devotees and powerful enemies. "The horrible Stigian smoke of the pit that is bottomelesse" James I of England had said in his 1604 *Counterblaste to Tobacco*. During that early period, smoking was damned as a foul-smelling, loathsome habit, harmful to the brain and lungs. Many medical practitioners inveighed against its use and set up demonstrations to illustrate its dangers. In 1665, Samuel Pepys witnessed a Royal Society experiment in which a cat quickly expired when fed "a drop of the distilled oil of tobacco." But the controversial leaf was also credited by some doctors with a fantastic list of therapeutic effects. Juan de Cardenas, a Spanish physician who lived in Mexico in the late sixteenth century, wrote that "Soldiers, subject to privations, keep off cold, hunger, and thirst by smoking," and that "All the inhabitants of the hot countries of the Indies alleviate their discomforts by the smoke of this blessed and medicinal plant." During the recurrent epidemics of plague in the seventeenth century, it was widely believed that smokers were spared, and men who attended the sick and went around with the deadcarts kept their pipes lit.

In pre-Columbian America, the medicinal uses of tobacco were numerous. Powdered tobacco mixed with lime was rubbed on the skin for tiredness and aching muscles. The Aztecs also mixed the leaf with lime and rubbed themselves with the mixture as a cure for gout. Ground tobacco was employed in some parts of South America as an intoxicant to enfeeble rattlesnakes and as a badge of office for women practitioners of midwifery, who would rub ground tobacco and lime on the arms of pregnant women to make them invulnerable to witchcraft. In Yucatan, tobacco was credited with the prevention of certain seizures, primarily mental disorders, and the Yucatec ethnobotany showed it as a remedy for such a wide range of complaints as asthma, chills, fevers, convulsions, sore eyes, bowel complaints, skin diseases, primary infections, and bites and stings.

A similar diversity of human ills and afflictions was treated with the magical tobacco in Europe after the middle of the sixteenth century. Portuguese traders, in particular, grew rich on the traffic in medicinal tobacco, which for a time was hailed as a cure for almost every known disease.

The scientific study of tobacco and its effects on the body may be said to have begun in 1671, when the Italian biologist, Francesco Redi, published an account of the lethal effects of the "oil of tobacco." But it was not until the early 1800's, probably about 1810, that Louis Nicolas

Vauquelin, a French chemist, identified the active principal ingredient in tobacco, which he called *"Nicotianine,"* after the French envoy who had introduced tobacco to the court of France some two and a half centuries earlier.

Vauquelin was not able to isolate the oil completely. More work remained to be done. Nicotine, a poisonous oily liquid, is now known to be one of the main substances of tobacco, which also contains starches, reducing sugars (such as dextrose), sucrose, cellulose, pectin, salts of various organic acids, resins, and nitrogen. Cigarette smoke is a mixture of gases, uncondensed vapors, and billions of tiny liquid particles. "Tobacco tar" is the chemists' shorthand for the composite of hundreds of distinct chemical compounds isolated or remaining to be isolated from condensed tobacco smoke. The smoke of one cigarette produces differing amounts of nicotine and tars, depending on the length of the cigarette, the paper, the kind of filter, if any, the tobacco type, and many other factors.

Early participants in the tobacco controversy did not associate its use with the production of cancer, although they did blame it for causing or curing almost every other known disease. Dr. John Hill, a well-known London physician, botanist, columnist, and playwright, first suggested a relation in 1761. Dr. Hill, a 1750 medical graduate of the Scottish University of St. Andrews, found that snuff was able to produce "swellings and excrescences." In a tract entitled *Cautions against the Immoderate Use of Snuff*, he reported six cases of "polypusses" related to the excessive use of snuff. One gentleman, described by Dr. Hill,

> after a long and immoderate use of Snuff, perceived that he breathed with difficulty through one of his nostrils: the

complaint gradually increased, 'till he perceived a swelling within, which was *hard*, but without *pain*. It grew slowly, 'till, in the end, it filled up that whole nostril, and swelled the nose so as to obstruct the breathing at the other: he found it necessary then to apply for assistance. The Swelling was quite black: it adhered by a broad base, so that it was impossible to attempt the getting it away, either by the knife or ligature: He had hitherto felt no great pain; but, while the people about him were deliberating what to do, he perceived an unconquerable itching in the lower part of it. His principal surgeon, who was a very skillful one, cautioned him most earnestly to avoid scratching it; but in vain: he could not forbear; and the consequence was a discharge of a thin sharp humour, with dreadful pain, and all the frightful symptoms of an open cancer. He tried the famous Hemlock, but without success: it produced no good nor ill effect in him, and he was without hope when I last saw him.

Another case described by Dr. Hill involved a lady "of sober and virtuous life" who nevertheless had taken a vast quantity of snuff and developed a terrible ulcer in the nose. "There was no cause to suspect the accidents which sometimes bring on the worst ulcers in that part of the face," the doctor wrote in another of his horror stories.

She had been long accustomed to Snuff, and took it in very great quantity. After the use of about a quarter of a pound of Snuff, which she perceived to be particularly acrid; she felt a strange soreness in the upper part of her left nostril; running, as she expressed it, toward the gristle of the nose; she left off that particular parcel of Snuff, but continued to take the usual kind as much as ever. No swelling was perceived; but, after a little time came on a discharge of a very offensive matter; not in great quantity, but of an intolerable smell, and the more so to her, as she was naturally a person of great delicacy. The discharge increased, and it soon became necessary for her to leave off Snuff. A surgeon was employed, but to very little purpose; the symptoms continued; the ulcer increased, and, from time to time, pieces of the bone came away. Death, from another disease, put an end to that misery, which all the art of physick and surgery seemed very little able to relieve.

Dr. Hill reported four other "polypusses," including one of the esophagus, that he did not label as cancers or describe in enough detail to evaluate their malignancy. But he did make the following sophisticated comment:

Whether or not polypusses, which attend Snuff-takers, are absolutely caused by that custom; or whether the principles of the disorder were there before, and Snuff only irritated the parts, and hastened the mischief, I shall not pretend to determine: but even supposing the latter only to be the case, the damage is certainly more than the indulgence is worth: for who is able to say, that the Snuff is not the absolute cause, or that he has not the seeds of such a disorder which Snuff will bring into action. With respect to the cancer of the nose, they are as dreadful and as fatal as any others. . . . It is evident therefore that no man should venture Snuff, who is not sure that he is not so far liable to a cancer: and no man can be sure of that.

Sir Percivall Pott, another London physician, observed in 1775 the tragic frequency with which cancer of the scrotum occurred among chimney sweeps. It was his diagnosis that the cancers were caused by the sweeps' excessive contact with soot (a substance in which polycyclic hydrocarbons, or tars, are intimately involved). There were later discussions of tobacco and health in the *Lancet,* an English medical journal. One of the series of articles published in its 1857 symposium contended that "Tobacco is said to act on the mind by producing inactivity thereof; inability to think; drowsiness; irritability. . . .

On the respiratory organs, it acts by causing consumption, haemoptysis, and inflammatory condition of the mucous membrane of the larynx, trachea, and bronchae, ulceration of the larynx; short irritable cough; hurried breathing. The circulating organs are affected by irritable heart circulation."

The modern period of investigation into the question of smoking and health began about 1900, when an increase in what was by then recognized as cancer of the lungs was noted by vital statisticians. Their data are usually taken as the starting point for studies of the possible relationship of smoking and other uses of tobacco to cancer of the lungs and other organs, to diseases of the heart and blood vessels, and to diseases of the lower respiratory tract. Tobacco juice was the first tobacco product used to induce cancer in an experimental animal, and related studies of the development of skin cancer in guinea pigs were first reported in 1900. In 1925, the British chemist Sir Ernest L. Kennaway put match to virtually every organic substance he could lay his hands on—petroleum, coal, skin, hair, yeast, cholesterol—and in each case was able to produce cancerous tumors on the skins of laboratory animals by painting them with the condensed smoke "tar."

Little more than a decade later, a condemnation of tobacco-smoking came from an unexpected and prestigious source. Dr. Raymond Pearl, an eminent scientist and professor of biology at the Johns Hopkins Medical School in Baltimore, Maryland, came up with a very unfavorable comparison between the number of deaths among smokers and nonsmokers. In a 1938 report to the New York Academy of Medicine on "The Search for Longevity," he presented what he felt were the first life tables showing the reduced life expectancy of smokers. His tables also demonstrated that the reduction in longevity is proportional to the amount of tobacco used. "Smoking is associated with a definite impairment of longevity," he reported. "This impairment is proportional to the habitual amount of tobacco usage by smoking, being great for heavy smokers and less for moderate smokers." Of the 6,813 persons reported on, two-thirds of the nonsmokers had lived beyond sixty; 61 per cent of the moderate smokers had reached the same age; but only 46 per cent of the heavy smokers reached age sixty. At the same time, Dr. Pearl reported that he could find no relationship between moderate drinking and the life span. Under the title "Tobacco Smoking and Longevity," his findings were published in the March 4, 1938, issue of *Science*. *Time* magazine, which picked them up, suggested that they would frighten tobacco manufacturers to death and "make tobacco users' flesh creep."

But the average American, if he read the report, appeared to take more comfort from the item on alcohol than fright at the warning about tobacco. While Dr. Pearl commented on the amount of publicity his report received, saying that he had paid for many items from a clipping bureau, George Seldes, author of *Lords of the Press* (New York: J. Messner, 1938), argued that most of Pearl's clippings came from small-town papers, while the large metropolitan dailies, fattening on tobacco advertising, had either ignored or buried his report.

During the 1930's, the increase in lung cancer became the subject of intensive investigation among medical people. Dr. Morton L. Levin, of Buffalo, New York, began to specialize in the study of epidemiology of cancer in 1937. In that year, he also became associated with a special New York State commission to study cancer and served as director of the Bureau of Cancer Control of the New York State Department of Health. Dr. Levin, who later became head of the department of Epidemiology at the

Roswell Park Memorial Institute in Buffalo, started research on the possible relationship between cigarette-smoking and lung cancer after reading a German article on the first controlled retrospective study of smoking and lung cancer, F. H. Müller's famous *Tabakmissbrauch und Lungencarcinom,* published in 1939. Dr. Charles S. Cameron, who served as a Rockefeller Fellow at New York City's Memorial Hospital, a large cancer clinic, became interested in the smoking-cancer relationship in the mid-1930's. Dr. Richard H. Overholt, of Boston, who did postgraduate work in surgery at the University Hospital in Philadelphia, served as instructor in surgery at the University of Pennsylvania, and founded the Overholt Thoracic Clinic in Boston, became suspicious in the early 1940's that a connection existed between heavy smoking and lung cancer. He himself stopped smoking. Retrospective studies were published in 1943, 1945, and 1948—all of which reported some sort of link between smoking and cancer. Thereafter, the investigative pace quickened.

The upward movement of tobacco consumption had several different groups worried. Smoking caused fires, for one thing, with loss of life and property damages totaling hundreds of thousands of dollars a year—a matter of real concern to insurance companies, city officials, and others. And medical investigators continued to produce research indicating that smoking was definitely bad for some people. Experts at the Mayo Clinic cautioned against use of cigarettes by patients who suffered from peripheral vascular disease or arterial injury. Dr. Alton Ochsner, a New Orleans surgeon and regional medical director of the American Cancer Society, told an audience at Duke University on October 23, 1945, that he believed "there is a distinct parallelism between the incidence of cancer of the lung and the sale of cigarettes . . . the increase is due to the increased incidence of smoking and that smoking is a factor because of the chronic irritation it produces." Former heavyweight champion Gene Tunney, then a lieutenant commander in charge of U.S. Navy physical training, wrote an article for the *Reader's Digest* in December, 1941, entitled "Nicotine Knockout, or the Slow Count." "You do get a 'lift' when you light a cigarette," Tunney said. "But it's exactly like the lift you get from cocaine, heroin, marijuana." The *Reader's Digest* was to become a thorn in the side of the tobacco industry.

While the public paid little attention to the early health warnings, possibly because they were based on data contained in mortality and personal medical records rather than first-hand experience with human beings, tobacco men could not help but feel a sense of dark foreboding. Almost instinctively, they fell back on their old friend advertising. Right up to his death in 1946, George Washington Hill had been convinced that the impetus of such "great advertising campaigns," as that he had led for American Tobacco's Lucky Strike had built the cigarette business. (So complete was Hill's identification with his product that he grew tobacco plants in the garden of his home and radios in every room bathed him in the sound of his own cigarette commercials.) Other early leaders in the cigarette business were equally convinced that advertising had had a profound influence on the consumption of their product. *Printer's Ink,* the advertising trade journal, claimed that advertising was the one feature that contributed more than any other to the growth of the industry. In *The Economic Effects of Advertising* (Chicago: Richard D. Irwin, 1942), Professor Neil Borden of the Harvard Business School wrote that: "without advertising, cigarette use would probably have grown; with advertising, the increase has been amazing."

Quite naturally, then, in response to what industry spokesmen referred to as "the health scare," the cigarette advertisers began to sell health. To counter Old Gold's "Not a Cough in a Carload!," Camel came up with "Not a Single Case of Throat Irritation Due to Smoking Camels," and Philip Morris boasted that it was "The Throat-Tested Cigarette." Harking back to the sixteenth-century Portuguese pharmacology, cigarettes were promoted as a tonic for all manner of ills. Was your stomach troubling you? "For digestion's sake, smoke Camels . . . stimulates the flow of digestive fluids . . . increases alkalinity." A white-frocked medical man on the back cover of magazines confided that "More doctors smoke Camels than any other cigarette."

The American Medical Association (AMA) took note of the identification of smoking with doctors and, terming it "a cheap attempt to mislead" the public, banned cigarette ads from its own publications. On another front, the industry encountered resistance to its new promotional tactics. Some people in the Federal Trade Commission (FTC) were concerned about the health question, and the agency's jurisdiction over unfair and deceptive practices brought it into the picture. Julep, a now-defunct brand of cigarettes, claimed to be a remedy for coughs; the commission asked the manufacturers, Penn Tobacco Company, to stop making that claim. A 1942 complaint against Brown & Williamson prohibited claims that Kools would keep the head clear or give extra protection against colds. The FTC continued to attack until it built an impressive court record upholding its position against health and medical claims for cigarette smoking.

In a leading case, *P. Lorillard Co.* v. *FTC*, the company was charged by the FTC with making a distorted use of a *Reader's Digest* article that discussed the harmful effects of various brands of cigarettes. A laboratory had concluded that no particular brand of cigarettes was substantially more harmful than any other. A table of variations in brand characteristics was inserted in the article to show the insignificance of the differences that existed in the tar and nicotine content of the smoke produced by the various brands. The table indicated that Old Golds had less nicotine and tars, although the difference was so small as to be insignificant. Lorillard launched a national advertising campaign stressing that the *Reader's Digest* test proved that its brand was "lowest in nicotine and tars," and defended its advertising before the FTC on the ground that it had truthfully reported what had been stated in the article. In a 1950 decision, the Fourth Circuit Court of Appeals, upholding the commission's cease-and-desist order, declared that Lorillard's advertising violated the FTC Act because, by printing only a small part of the article, it created an entirely false and misleading impression. "To tell less than the whole truth is a well-known method of deception," the court ruled.

In another case, against Liggett & Myers, the FTC tested the question of whether cigarettes fall under the food and drug sections of the Federal Trade Commission Act, which, by 1938 amendment, provide for preliminary injunctions, impose criminal penalties, and broaden the commission's jurisdiction over sellers where false and deceptive advertiisng of food, drugs, and cosmetics is concerned. The U.S. District Court for the Southern District of New York decided that cigarettes do not fall within the definition of food, drugs, or cosmetics, although they are used in intimate contact with the body. Sellers were, therefore, not required to disclose the consequences of use where failure to disclose would be deceptive. Many persons have felt that, for one reason or another, cigarette advertising should not be subject to these special provisions. But if cigarettes are not foods, drugs, or cosmetics, what are they? Simply a commodity in trade?

As U.S. laws are presently constituted, there is no government agency with clear jurisdiction over the health aspects of cigarettes. The Federal Trade Commission can act on matters of advertising and package information. The Food and Drug Administration (FDA) concerns itself only with foods, drugs, solids, or liquids that are eaten or drunk. Tobacco is neither a food nor a drug, under current legal definitions. Nor are cigarettes eaten or drunk; they are inhaled. The 1890 edition of the *U.S. Pharmacopoeia,* an official listing of drugs published by the government, included tobacco. In later editions, tobacco was dropped. Former Senator Maurine Neuberger (D., Oregon) has claimed that the removal of tobacco from the *Pharmacopoeia* was the price paid to get support of tobacco-state legislators for the Food and Drug Act of 1906. The leaf was thereby removed from the jurisdiction of the FDA.

Cigarette-smoking increased dramatically from 1930 onward in the United States, but statistics show that it made its greatest percentage gains during the years of World War II and the rapid urbanization that accompanied and immediately followed the war. In 1945, some 267 billion cigarettes were sold on the domestic market, an increase of 12 per cent over 1944, 48 per cent over 1940, 124 per cent over 1930. Demand appeared to be insatiable. During World War II, long lines formed outside tobacco shops, and 18 per cent of cigarette output during 1941–45 (or 222.6 billion cigarettes) was sent overseas. Because of the leaf shortage, President Roosevelt classified tobacco as an essential crop, draft boards were directed to defer tobacco farmers to ensure maximum output, and some women smokers patriotically took to the pipe. G.I.'s in

Europe used cigarettes as barter. After the war, cigarettes for a time became the most stable currency in Germany, France, and Italy.

As time went on, there were more and more smokers of ten, fifteen and twenty years' duration in the general public. Men who had begun to smoke in the service kept up the habit in civilian life. Many women, who had taken up the habit or smoked more during the war, also found themselves hooked. Some of these smokers began to complain to their family doctors about persistent coughing, difficulty in breathing, open sores in the mouth, chronic bronchitis, or worse. And further scientific evidence accumulated on the alleged harmful effects of cigarette-smoking.

In 1949, Dr. E. Cuyler Hammond, reporting to the American Cancer Society on trends in cancer mortality, pointed to a strong statistical connection between heavy cigarette-smoking and the incidence of lung cancer. Scientific studies were undertaken in many countries. The most elaborate of them in the United States by Dr. Hammond and Dr. Daniel Horn and, in England, by Dr. W. R. Doll and Dr. A. B. Hill, implicated cigarette-smoking as a factor intimately associated with lung cancer. In 1950, at the fifth International Cancer Research Congress in Paris, groups of scientists working independently maintained that cigarette inhalation was responsible for lung cancer, particularly among men who had smoked a pack a day for twenty years or more. But women smokers, it seemed, were rarely affected, and opponents of the theories linking smoking and cancer seized on this discrepancy as evidence that cancer of the lungs is caused by other factors.

In 1952, Liggett & Myers conducted a test to determine the effects of smoking Chesterfields on the nose, throat, and accessory organs. This seems, from available records, to have been the only such test undertaken during this period by a tobacco company. It was conducted by Arthur D. Little, Inc., in that research group's Cambridge, Massachusetts, testing laboratory, and its conclusion was that smoking Chesterfields had no harmful effect on the organs in question. The test was widely publicized and the results used to assure the general public that Chesterfields were harmless.

But real trouble for the tobacco industry had begun to loom. Dr. Ochsner had already published numerous articles in medical journals linking lung cancer and cigarette-smoking. In 1953, he stated, in the *Journal of the American Geriatrics Society* (Volume 1), his conviction that "the tremendous and unprecedented increase of the incidence of bronchogenic carcinoma in recent years is due to the carcinogenic effect of tobacco. Because of the likely causal relationship between cigarette smoking and bronchogenic carcinoma, it is our belief that all men who have smoked a package of cigarettes a day for twenty years are likely candidates for bronchogenic carcinoma."

Also, in that year, an article in *Cancer Research* reported on the results of a study of the possible carcinogenic effects of tobacco smoke by Dr. Ernest L. Wynder and Dr. Evarts Graham of the Sloan-Kettering Institute of Cancer Research in New York. These two scientists concluded that cancer could be induced on the skin of mice by tobacco-tar condensates. Another antismoking article, "Cancer by the Carton," appeared in *Reader's Digest*.

But if 1952 and 1953 were threatening years for the tobacco industry's image, the year 1954 was worse. It was a watershed in the history of smoking research. Studies had been made on mice. What about men?

Doctors Hammond and Horn of the American Cancer Society had for their investigative convenience a large population of 70 million people who willingly and regularly smoked. With the help of 22,000 trained volunteers, in January, 1952, they had enrolled 187,783 men between the ages of fifty and sixty-nine in a massive study. The smoking or nonsmoking habits of each man were precisely noted. Then the two researchers sat back and waited. On October 31, 1953, they took a preliminary look at the comparative death rates of smokers and nonsmokers. That look was so startling that Dr. Horn, previously a moderately heavy smoker, never smoked cigarettes again. (Today, he heads the federal government's antismoking campaign.) Of 11,870 men in the study group who had died, 7,316 were smokers. If the death rate of the smokers had been comparable to the death rate of the nonsmokers, only 4,651 would have died. The doctors concluded that the deaths of 2,265 smokers had to be considered as "excess deaths" and related to smoking. Coronary artery disease claimed more than half of these. Lung cancer took 14 per cent—as much as all other cancers. Also prominent among the causes of "excess deaths" were cancer of the larynx and the esophagus, gastric ulcers, pneumonia, and influenza.

The death rate of regular cigarette-smokers was generally 68 per cent higher than that of nonsmokers; that of smokers of two or more packs a day was 123 per cent higher. Cigar-smokers had only a 22 per cent higher death rate, while the pipe-smokers escaped relatively unscathed with a death rate only 12 per cent in excess of nonsmokers.

Of the total 127 deaths from cancer of the mouth, tongue, lip, larynx, pharynx, and esophagus, only four occurred in men who never smoked. Here, pipe- and cigar-smokers came into the statistical picture. Their death rates from these diseases were also far higher than those of the nonsmokers, apparently because the reduced alkalinity of smoke from Virginia leaf used in cigarettes enables the smoker to inhale more freely without coughing, whereas pipe and cigar smoke is far more alkaline and harder to inhale. Pipe and cigar tobaccos generally produce more tar and nicotine, but these substances are not usually sucked into the lungs where they may irritate tissues or be transmitted to the bloodstream.

In absolute numbers, heart disease claimed the most victims among the smokers. But the ratio of smoker lung-cancer fatalities to nonsmoker fatalities was the most startling statistic of all. Deaths from lung cancer were ten times as frequent in smokers as in nonsmokers. Even more startling, the chances of the heavy smoker dying of lung cancer were found to be sixty-four times that of the non-smoker. A very important finding was that ex-smokers had significantly lower death rates than those who continued to smoke regularly. The longer the ex-smoker abstained, the more his death rate resembled that of the nonsmoker.

On June 21, 1954, the American Cancer Society gave a report of the Hammond-Horn study to a meeting of the American Medical Association in San Francisco. Released to the public, the findings made a strong impact. The tobacco industry has never been quite the same since.

♣ 6

The Filtered Fifties

WHEN THE QUESTION of smoking and health became a matter of general public discussion in 1953, the industry plunged into a state of ulcerous tension. For the first time in twenty-one years, the upward curve of cigarette sales, impervious to wars and depression, leveled off and declined slightly. Over the two-year period 1953–54, total consumption declined 6.4 per cent and per capita consumption declined 8.8 per cent. While the "Eisenhower boom" sent stock-market prices spiraling to new highs, tobacco shares wavered at previous levels. Publicity attending the mounting evidence of serious health hazards in smoking is the only factor that has ever been suggested to explain these declines.

The situation was sufficiently perturbing to induce the major tobacco manufacturing and handling companies to take full-page display ads in the press at the beginning of 1954. These ads said that while the industry had full confidence that its products were not injurious to health, it was "pledging aid and assistance to the research effort into all phases of tobacco use and health," and had set up a Tobacco Industry Research Committee (TIRC), to be directed by "a scientist of unimpeachable integrity and

national repute," which would have available the services of "an Advisory Board of Scientists disinterested in
the cigarette industry." The man named scientific director
of TIRC—later renamed the Council for Tobacco Re-
search-U.S.A.—was Dr. Clarence Cook Little, an eminent
geneticist and cancer specialist, who at the time of his
appointment was director of the Roscoe B. Jackson Memorial Laboratory at Bar Harbor, Maine, and who had for-
merly been managing director of the American Society for
Control of Cancer, the predecessor of the American Cancer
Society. The TIRC was to sponsor research into questions
of tobacco and health and to "communicate authoritative
factual information on the subject to the public." The
manufacturers were to support this research. This brain-
child was delivered of Hill and Knowlton, the resourceful
public relations firm of international fame. Although research money was to be awarded with no strings attached,
the TIRC nicely served the purpose of identifying the
industry with the welfare of humanity and spreading good
will through the scientific community.

But bad news continued to come in from the scientific
front. After 1954, a great quantity of new research was
published, almost all of which tended to show that cigarette-smoking is a causative factor in lung cancer and other
diseases. The U.S. Public Health Service (PHS) became
officially engaged in an appraisal of the available data on
smoking and health in June, 1956, when, at the instigation
of the Surgeon General, a scientific study group was set up
to make a comprehensive review of the evidence. The
group, put together by the National Cancer Institute, the
National Heart Institute, the American Cancer Society,
and the American Heart Association, appraised sixteen
independent studies carried on in five countries over a
period of eighteen years and concluded that there is a

causal relationship between excessive smoking of cigarettes and lung cancer. On March 6, 1957, it issued a report that said: "The evidence of cause-effect relationship is adequate for considering the initiation of public health measures." The British Medical Research Council completed a comprehensive review of the evidence in June, 1957. Its conclusions were similar. And in July, 1957, U.S. Surgeon General Dr. Leroy Burney declared: "The Public Health Service feels the weight of the evidence is increasingly pointing in one direction: that excessive smoking is one of the causative factors in lung cancer." In a special article entitled "Smoking and Lung Cancer—A Statement of the Public Health Service," published in the *Journal* of the American Medical Association on November 28, 1959, Dr. Burney reiterated that belief.

The manufacturers had to do something. The "health scare" led to the revival of the filter cigarette favored by Russian aristocrats and New Yorkers in the old days. The filter brands evolved from the so-called "mouthpiece" cigarette, dating back to the nineteenth century, which had a stiff paper tube extending from the tobacco column containing a tuft of cotton. These filters were not easy to make; such brands as Tolstoi and Svoboda were expensive specialities. The premium-priced Parliament introduced by Benson & Hedges in 1932 had such a mouthpiece. But popular-priced filter brands were very much the exception before the 1950's.

Brown & Williamson had a filter brand, Viceroy, on the market. Sixteen years after its introduction in 1936, it represented less than 8 per cent of B & W sales. But during the 1950's, Viceroy lifted its company out of the marginal category. First on the filter scene at popular prices, Viceroy was the leading filter brand through 1954. In that year, B & W changed the filter from a hollow tube with cotton to a tip of cellulose acetate—a material that quickly became the "normal" filter throughout he industry.

The filter was the principal device used by merchandisers to reassure smokers. By switching to filter-tip cigarettes, smokers could allay their fears while holding onto their habit. Publicity, particularly a 1954 article in *Reader's Digest,* on the Hammond-Horn report gave filters a great sales boost. Kent, the first filter cigarette to be promoted in a big way (it enjoyed a sudden popularity directly attributable to the *Reader's Digest* story), had been put on the market in 1952 at a premium price by Lorillard, which was not doing as well as it wished with Old Gold even the year before trouble started. The function of a filter was presumably to trap condensates, including nicotine and tars from cigarette smoke. The Kent "micronite" filter was said to subject the smoker to 50 per cent less tar and nicotine than the average, contemporary, nonfilter cigarettes. In a clear response to the "health scare," Kent said that its filter "takes out more nicotine and tars than any other leading cigarette—the difference in protection is priceless." But after an initial spurt, sales of Kent proved disappointing. Smokers found it hard to draw smoke through the filter. In 1957, Lorillard found it necessary to change the filter design and more than double the nicotine content of Kents while nearly doubling the tar content.

Filters proved a convenience as well as a presumed safeguard. They eliminated loose tobacco ends and afforded the smoker a firmer purchase between the lips. Since filters were less expensive than the tobacco they replaced, manufacturers were not reluctant to enter the race to create and promote new filter brands. Some manufacturers saw filters as their salvation. Lorillard's competitors went to work developing filters to compete with Kent's. As demand rose, filter brands multiplied. In 1953, Liggett & Myers brought out L & M, with a "Pure White Miracle Tip of Alpha-Cellulose" described as "just what the doctor ordered." Reynolds put out Winston, which "filters so effectively." American had its cork-tipped, king-size Herbert Tareyton. But it was now given a "new Selective Filter," with "an entirely new concept in cigarette filtration—a filter tip of purified cellulose, incorporating Activated Charcoal, a filtering substance world famous as a purifying agent." Old Golds came out in a filter version. There was now a three-way cigarette split: regular, nonfilter king, and filter. Other splits followed: Kools and Raleighs came out with filters. Then Philip Morris bought out Benson & Hedges to get Parliament and developed a filter cigarette of its own from an old property, Marlboro, which was dressed up with a cellulose acetate filter trade-named "Selectrate" and packed in a hinged "flip-top" or crush-proof box. The "tar derby" was in full swing. Cigarette sales, instead of entering a permanent decline after a two-year drop, moved up again.

By this time, the selling of the cigarette had entered into a new phase. Tobacco manufacturers were pouring more and more money into television advertising. From about $40 million in 1957, they increased spending on TV to about $115 million in 1961. Squads of beautiful girls and virile young men, water skiers, pilots, speedboat racers—you name it—had been let loose on the home screen in the tobacco industry's frenzied efforts to overcome the bad news from medical circles. Brand image was the big thing, and motivational research had become the byword on Madison Avenue. In 1956, the Cigar Institute decided to demasculinize the cigar to appeal to women. Now, with the help of market research, Philip Morris went all out to give Marlboro a male-oriented image. A rugged rancher type who had come up the hard way and got tattooed somewhere along the line, he was the brooding smoker in "Marlboro country."

By the mid-1950's, cigarette advertising shouted conflicting claims for cigarettes that were low, lower, and lowest in tar and nicotine. The Federal Trade Commission had by then chalked up an impressive series of court decisions upholding its right to protect consumers against claims that smoking is somehow beneficial to health or helps weight-reducing. In 1952, the FTC had worked itself into a fury at Liggett & Myers, whose Chesterfield had once been its darling among tobacco advertisers because it contented itself with the simple slogan "They Satisfy." Following lengthy litigation, words like "milder" and "smoother" had been stricken from the cigarette ad man's vocabulary. For nearly a decade, the FTC had battled Chesterfield's competitors, until binding cease-and-desist orders had been nailed down on therapeutic claims. Now, the FTC was outraged to discover that Liggett & Myers was switching to Chesterfield claims prohibited for other companies and went to court to seek a preliminary injunction barring the new ads. But the U.S. District Court for the Southern District of New York denied the injunction. Finally, after six years of litigation, during the course of which an FTC examiner's finding that "milder" and "smoother" were "puffery" was overturned by the five-member commission, Liggett & Myers was also placed under a cease-and-desist order. But in the light of the growing scientific data that questioned the healthfulness of cigarettes, the FTC action seemed puny. Consumption of cigarettes was increasing, especially among young people, and the agency attributed the increase to advertising.

In 1955, the FTC broadened its attack on cigarette advertising. In September of that year, it issued some guides that prohibited either stated or implied medical approval of smoking in general or any cigarette in particular. Unsubstantiated claims about nicotine, tars, or other components were also barred. After the guides were issued, the FTC began to monitor all cigarette advertising. But there were ways to modify ads so as to imply that smoking was a healthful activity without actually saying so. To the chagrin of the FTC, these commercials did not run afoul of the law. A health warning was needed, but in the absence of a government position on the health question, this was not possible.

Feelings in the industry were running high. Loyalties were being tested. One case of internecine fighting involved *Reader's Digest,* which for twenty-eight years had been a faithful client of the New York advertising agency Batten, Barton, Durstine, and Osborn. Also prominent in the BBD&O stable of clients was the American Tobacco Company, whose estimated annual advertising expenditures of $22 million overshadowed the *Digest's* paltry $1.25 million. The July, 1957, issue of *Reader's Digest* contained an article discussing the state of the medical evidence against smoking, with particular reference to the filter tip. On July 17, 1957, BBD&O resigned its contract with *Reader's Digest.*

For years, certain members of Congress had worked to introduce legislation to restrict the sale of cigarettes, convey health warnings, or regulate cigarette advertising in one way or another. A number of bills had been introduced. One of them, sponsored by Senator Richard Neuberger (D., Oregon), would have removed tobacco from the list of basic crops supported by the Department of Agriculture. (The Commodity Credit Corporation, created in 1933 to finance price-support and production-stabilization programs for wheat, corn, cotton, peanuts, rice, soybeans, and tobacco, among other crops, to encourage production adjustments, and to maintain farm income by making payments for diverting cropland from the production of these commodities, was made part of the Department of Agriculture in 1939.) But none of the bills had ever been given a hearing.

In 1957, Representative John A. Blatnik (D., Minnesota), chairman of the Legal and Monetary Subcommittee of the Government Operations Committee, conducted hearings to define the responsibility of the FTC regarding advertising claims for filter cigarettes. The Blatnik subcommittee provided a forum for a discussion of the health question. Both sides were given an airing. Some scientists, including the chief medical statistician of the Mayo Clinic and a Yale pathologist, held the cancer theory suspect because of lack of pathological or biographical evidence. An American Medical Association cancer-research-committee chairman testified that a human would have to smoke 100,000 cigarettes a day to get an equivalent exposure of tar used in experiments that produced skin cancer on mice. A New York professor of medicine said that while the relative percentage of women cigarette-smokers was increasing, the incidence of female lung cancer was decreasing. It was pointed out that dogs showed an increase in lung cancer but no increase in cigarette-smoking. Dr. Clarence Cook Little of the Tobacco Industry Research Committee, asked to comment on filter tips, replied that to him filters were a matter of "complete and unenthusiastic indifference."

But other witnesses reiterated the adverse medical findings. Surgeon General Leroy Burney told the group: "It is clear there is an increasing and consistent body of evidence that excessive cigarette smoking is one of the causative factors in lung cancer." Dr. John R. Heller, Director of the National Cancer Institute, testified that the "overwhelming majority" of scientists and physicians in the

Public Health Service supported this position. He also estimated that 75 per cent of physicians and scientists "who have knowledge and some competence within this area" would also support the stand of the Surgeon General.

Researchers at the Roswell Park Memorial Institute had found benefits in filters—such as an absence of coughing and shortness of breath in smokers who used them. Extracting tar from four brands of unfiltered and two brands of filtered cigarettes to apply to the skin of laboratory mice, the Roswell Park doctors found that filtered cigarettes produced a third less tar than nonfiltered brands. When the question of filters and their effectiveness came up in the Blatnik hearings, Dr. Ernest Wynder, of Sloan-Kettering, testified:

> It is feasible to produce filter tips with a satisfactory pressure drop and satisfactory flavor, which can remove about 40 per cent of the tar of the cigarette smoke. Such a filter incorporated in a regular-size cigarette, which normally yields 30 milligrams of tar in its smoke, can reduce the tar exposure of a given individual smoking this cigarette to about 18 milligrams. A reduction to such level, as animal experiments as well as the human statistical studies show, will be followed by a significant reduction in cancer risk, provided, of course, that the number of cigarettes smoked is kept constant.

But FTC Chairman John Gwynne cast a shadow over the ultimate value of filters, saying:

> We have completed a consumer survey conducted for the purpose of determining primarily what results smokers expect from smoking filter-tip cigarettes. In the course of the survey, the Commission's Bureau of Investigation interviewed smokers of filter-tip cigarettes in widely scattered

areas of the country who smoke over 10 cigarettes a day. . . . As to the comparative number of cigarettes smoked a day, more than half said they smoked the same number while approximately 30 per cent said they smoked more filter tips.

On the floor of the Senate, Senator Maurine Neuberger, citing industry efforts to curb antismoking campaigns in the schools, said there was one theme that runs through all cigarette advertising: "Today's adolescents are tomorrow's addicts." Yet, she added, despite its

cynical manipulation of symbols in an effort to boost sales figures, some tobacco interests have the temerity to criticize efforts to present another view of cigarette smoking. One can almost picture the counterpart of these tobacco spokesmen at the time of Pasteur's discovery of the relationship between fermentation in liquids and the growth of bacteria, a discovery which resulted in the development of pasteurization of milk and is today regarded as a giant forward step in the battle to protect human health.

In the House of Representatives, the tobacco industry for the most part spoke through its friends. North Carolina and Virginia congressmen would frequently insert in the *Congressional Record* speeches by tobacco company officials or by scientists who did not believe smoking can cause lung cancer.

Congressman Blatnik himself, during the course of the hearings, said that although his physicians had warned him against smoking, he had not given up cigarettes and enjoyed them. (Some years later, he underwent stomach surgery and stopped smoking.) But his testimonial did not soothe angry feelings in the tobacco industry when the subcommittee came out with its report in 1958 concluding that: "The cigarette manufacturers have deceived the American public through their advertising of cigarettes."

The report said that several of the best-selling filter cigarettes actually produced greater quantities of tar and nicotine than nonfilters, thereby preserving an illusion of safety while making sure their cigarette tasted "good like a cigarette should." Information on filters, based on laboratory tests conducted by Consumers Union, revealed that, in some cases, smokers who switched from regular to filter cigarettes were actually taking in greater amounts of tar and nicotine. A smoker of Lorillard's Old Golds, for example, who switched to Lorillard's Kent in 1953 would have cut down on such intake. But had he done so in 1957, he would have been inhaling more tar and nicotine. The same thing applied to smokers of Reynolds's Camels who switched to the same company's Winstons: they would have been increasing the amounts of tar and nicotine inhaled. The subcommittee's report concluded that:

> The Federal Trade Commission has failed in its statutory duty to "prevent deceptive acts or practices" in filter-cigarette advertising. The activities of the Commission to prevent this deception were weak and tardy. As a result, the connection between filter-tip cigarettes and "protection" has become deeply embedded in the public mind. The Federal Trade Commission has failed to approach the problems of false and misleading advertising with vigor and diligence. The members of the Commission should therefore immediately critically study the organizational structure of the Commission, its procedures and its personnel, and take such action as will insure that the Commission will be able to promptly and effectively prevent deceptive practices and misleading advertising.

Following this slap on the wrist, the FTC called an industry conference to work out a standard testing procedure for tar and nicotine content. A plan was developed, and the FTC duly shipped off identical unmarked cartons of cigarettes to several laboratories for testing. When the results came back, they were so inconsistent that the agency decided no reliable test existed.

Shortly after its report came out, the Blatnik subcommittee was reorganized out of existence by Representative William L. Dawson (D., Illinois), chairman of the full committee, though further hearings had been scheduled. A bill to regulate cigarette advertising, which included a suggestion that Congress set acceptable tar and nicotine levels, was never heard from again. According to Dawson, the first Negro ever to chair a congressional committee, a maximum of five subcommittees was necessary for efficient functioning of the committee. Representative Blatnik had the impression, however, that the subcommittee may have been declared "excess" by pressuring congressmen from tobacco states. Other sources, of the usual high-placed Washington sort, hazarded the opinion that Dawson abolished the subcommittee because of its criticism of U.S. aid programs and the progress of land reform in Vietnam—in other words, areas entirely unrelated to tobacco. Whatever the case, Congressman Blatnik had ventured into dangerous territory.

Innovations in filtration continued. "High filtration" was a term adopted in 1957 to mean substantial reduction in delivered smoke solids. But what was the consumer to do? If he followed the cigarette ads as a source of information, he would be, in the words of a January 24, 1958, *Wall Street Journal* article, "utterly confused." "Philip Morris says its new Parliament filter has '30,000 filaments.' Liggett & Myers Tobacco Company's television commercials talk about its L & M miracle tip with United States patent number 2,805,671. To say nothing of Hit Parade's '40,000 filter traps'!"

The tar derby continued unabated. The FTC guides may have had some effect in eliminating health claims from cigarette advertising, but they had little effect on tar and nicotine claims. Filter brands included regular and king sizes as well as mentholated smokes, which had quickly become the fastest-growing segment of the industry after Salem, in 1956, combined a menthol flavoring with a filter tip, and sales began to increase. Mentholated cigarettes were promoted as "cool" or "fresh," and millions of smokers switched. There were sharp increases in expenditures on television advertising for brands such as Newport, Salem, Alpine, Belair. Apparently, many smokers were convinced that filter and menthol-filter cigarettes were less hazardous to health than regular cigarettes. In 1952, only 1.5 per cent of the cigarettes sold in this country had filters. By 1956, filter-tip sales had ballooned to 30 per cent of the market, and by 1958, filter-tip brands rose to 46 per cent of sales. Mentholated brands accounted for about one in every six filter cigarettes smoked and one-twelfth of the total cigarette market.

While the reaction of men in the industry to the health question had not been uniform, it was thought best to keep internal dissension behind closed doors. Chinks had appeared in the industry's armor. There were signs of insubordination against American and Reynolds, which held the position that development of filters implied a health problem. Rothman's of Canada had taken a full-page ad in a Canadian newspaper to acknowledge the conclusiveness of evidence against smoking while touting its filter-tip Pall Mall. Other companies—Lorillard, for one—had devoted considerable effort to developing an effective filter. In 1958, a trade organization, the Tobacco Institute, was created to speak with one voice for the industry. The presidents of fourteen major tobacco-producers were to sit on its board, and it was to be financed by contributions from these large corporations according to their share of the market. The Institute set about to discredit anti-smoking publicity and project an image of tobacco as an American institution as old as Jamestown. The line was pushed that since there was no proof of any hazard in smoking, there was no need for safer cigarettes. George V. Allen, a respected career diplomat who was director of the U.S. Information Agency during the Eisenhower Administration, was chosen to head the Institute. He made speeches in which he argued that while statistical studies pointed to the need for further research, the questions about smoking and health remained unanswered. But more important, the Institute had enough economic and political power to meet the threat of the disorganized health groups, which had neither leadership nor adequate financial means to build an effective lobbying organization.

The "filtered fifties" ended on an ironic note. The FTC was still at work, but this time the regulatory agency stumbled badly. Efforts to deal with cigarette advertising on a company-by-company basis had proved ineffective. Weary of deciding the legal merits of individual claims, the FTC decided to knock the tar and nicotine out of cigarette advertising altogether. It moved in that direction by sending a letter to manufacturers on December 17, 1959: "We wish to advise that all representations of low or reduced tar or nicotine, whether by filtration or otherwise, will be construed as health claims. . . . Our purpose is to eliminate from cigarette advertising representations which in any way imply health benefit." In 1960, the commission announced that as a result of negotiation with industry, seven major manufacturers had agreed to abandon tar and nicotine claims. FTC Chairman Earl Kintner, an Eisenhower appointee, hailed the action as a landmark in industry-government cooperation.

But the new agreement also suited a powerful element in the industry that had been uneasy about the implied admission of potential harm in smoking involved in the development of filters. The FTC's action to end the "tar derby" had an unintended effect. It lessened incentive to produce a more effective filter. Sales of nonfilter cigarettes stopped their decline. Filters were disparaged in advertising with such innuendos as "Smoking more now but enjoying it less?" Nonfilter cigarettes began to imply safety with such words as "mildness," "gentleness," and "freshness." Pall Mall even claimed that its greater length acted as a sort of filter. The familiar mazes of charts and graphs disappeared from advertising copy, but Parliament promised an "extra margin." Extra margin of what? Safety, of course. To make sure no one missed the message, Parliament ads featured life-preservers, parachutes, a stunt diver's protective padding, and a fencer's mask. Unable to make capital on their relative safety, the high-filtration brands had a struggle just to stay alive. Some dropped out of sight.

🌿 7

Tobacco on Trial

FRANK LARTIGUE WAS A SMALL MAN, only five feet, four inches in height. He weighed less than 125 pounds. When he was a boy of nine in Louisiana in "about 1899," as his wife recalled he had said, he took up cigarette-smoking. At the time, the early antitrust storms were swirling around the tobacco industry. "Eatin' tobacco" had reached its per capita peak consumption in the United States some ten years earlier. By 1910, "the little tube of mighty power," the cigarette, was on the way up in popular esteem. By then Frank had been smoking for eleven years, sometimes rolling his own. A young man could roll about thirty-three "handmades" from a nickel sack of cigarette tobacco in those days.

In 1914, Frank Lartigue met Victoria St. Pierre, a Louisiana girl, and they were married three years later. For some years, they lived in Beaumont, Texas, where Frank made a living in the insurance business. But in about 1934, he began to suffer from rheumatic pains, and the couple moved to Hot Springs, Arkansas, where Frank could take the baths. While they lived in Hot Springs, he earned a living by selling magazine subscriptions. After that, he began traveling for a finance company as a debt collector. His wife took him on his rounds, because he didn't know how to drive an automobile. Together they traveled Louisiana, Texas, Arkansas, and Oklahoma. "Many times during the winter, I had to lower the windows in the automobile because of the smoke," Mrs. Lartigue said later.

Frank Lartigue died of lung cancer on July 13, 1955, at the age of 65. His wife, an aging, modest widow, who would normally have retired quietly to live with her sister in Houston, took another course of action and made a place for herself in history. Not a glorious place, perhaps, but certainly a place in the annals of medicine and the law.

The trial began on a muggy day in March, 1958. There was nothing distinctive about the appearance of the old Post Office building near Lee Circle in downtown New Orleans, a utilitarian product of New Deal days. But every seat in the federal courtroom inside was filled. Mrs. Lartigue three years earlier had filed a suit charging that the use of tobacco had caused the death of her husband. She was asking two major tobacco companies, R. J. Reynolds and Liggett & Myers, for $779,500 in damages. The trial was to bring before a jury for the first time the leading opponents of cigarette-smoking. Dr. Alton Ochsner, founder of the Ochsner cancer clinic and an outspoken proponent of the theory linking cigarette-smoking with lung cancer, headed the list of fifty prospective witnesses. Many of Dr. Ochsner's students from Tulane Medical School were among the spectators. Other physicians, surgeons, and researchers from as far away as Canada and Australia were due to appear. Now, for the first time, these authorities would be subjected to questioning by some of the nation's best legal brains, foreshadowing a debate that would continue for many years.

Shortly before 10 A.M. on the morning of March 23, the bailiff called the court to order and requested the public to stand. Federal Judge Herbert W. Christenberry entered the courtroom and took his place on the bench. A thin, soft-spoken man with a scholarly face, who was later to become chief judge of the U.S. District Court for the Eastern District of Louisiana, he began proceedings in the usual manner with selection of jurors.

Two days later, a headline in the *New Orleans Item* announced: JURY PANEL QUIZZED JUDGE RULES MISTRIAL. During a brief noon-hour recess, one of the eleven jurors told the judge that he had been contacted by a person claiming to be conducting a smoking survey. William W. Gardner, a postal clerk who had been accepted as a juror, said he received a telephone call from a woman who asked if he smoked. "I said 'no,' " Gardner told the judge. "She said 'thank you,' and hung up. Two minutes later, a lady called and asked for my age and if I was married. She said it was part of a Loyola survey." Seven other jurors then revealed that they had also been telephoned about their smoking habits. At the end of the recess, Judge Christenberry told the court he was astounded that so many prospective members of the federal jury panel had been contacted. "I will leave no stone unturned to find the culprit," he said. "Anyone tampering with a jury is culpable."

Judge Christenberry ordered a mistrial when it was revealed that one of Mrs. Lartigue's two lawyers, a former Louisiana state senator, H. Alva Brumfield, who walked with a limp and at the time sported a mottled red, black, and gray beard, had hired an investigator to gather information about the prospective jurors. Earl James Dominquez, former chief of detectives in Baton Rouge and later operator of a private investigative agency in

New Orleans, was called to appear in court. Judge Christenberry warned him before he took the stand that any testimony he gave might incriminate him and reminded him of the protection of the Fifth Amendment. But Dominquez refused this protection, saying he was willing to testify. While conceding that he had been hired by attorney Brumfield, the investigator said he had been told not to contact the prospective jurors themselves. He said he had turned over part of the investigation to his sister, Mary Teresa Michelli, who was to question neighbors of the prospective jurors. He denied knowing that she had gotten any information from jurors directly. More than twenty-two prospective jurors then revealed they had been contacted by a man or a woman, and that some of the callers said they were making a smoking survey for Loyola University.

"I do not believe you," Christenberry told Dominquez, according to a United Press account in the *New Orleans Item*, March 24, 1958. "The story he tells is incredible. This civil action cannot be tried before this jury panel. I am satisfied the witness [Dominquez] fully intended contacting jurors. It is clear to the court that the parties who called were the investigator and his sister. Regardless of whether or not a criminal offense has been committed, it will be referred to the proper authorities by the court."

The judge pointed out, however, that Brumfield and his colleague, the well-known San Francisco attorney Melvin M. Belli, had assured him that the investigator had been specifically instructed not to contact the prospective jurors themselves. After the mistrial, the judge announced that the case would be placed at the bottom of the docket and set for trial "when it reaches its turn." It seemed plain to all observers that attorneys Brumfield and Belli were interested in opening up a new field for litigation. Later, Belli, who was to become a national figure when he handled the defense of Jack Ruby for the shooting of Lee Harvey Oswald, accused murderer of President John F. Kennedy, took several similar cigarette-cancer cases in other parts of the country. He and Brumfield filed another suit in New Orleans a few months after the *Lartigue* mistrial, in which one Albert B. Hudson claimed that two products of R. J. Reynolds—Camels and Prince Albert tobacco—had caused his cancer of the larynx and vocal cords.

More than two years later, when the *Lartigue* case had worked its way up from the bottom of the docket, the widow Lartigue, Judge Christenberry, and a half-dozen lawyers must have experienced a strong feeling of *déjà vu*. They found themselves in the same courtroom on September 19, 1960, with virtually the same cast of characters. In addition to the plaintiff's attorneys, there were the same attorneys for the tobacco firms—two New Orleans firms backed up by the New York firm of Davis Polk Wardwell Sunderland & Kiendl (now Davis Polk & Wardwell), representing R. J. Reynolds. This time, Judge Christenberry excused a number of prospective jurors when they said that they had definite opinions on cancer and smoking. Among the first twelve called for questioning from a panel of thirty-eight there were six nonsmokers and three persons who said that they had smoked but had quit. Anticipating a lengthy trial, the judge asked jurors whether they had important business matters which would have to be attended to within the following two weeks. One was excused for that reason. The selection of twelve jurors, seven of them smokers, consumed the whole of the first day in court. The next day, after two alternate jurors were selected, Judge Christenberry instructed the attorney Brumfield to proceed with his opening statement for the plaintiff, Mrs. Lartigue.

Brumfield, sometimes referred to by Belli as "the king-fish," told the court that the two tobacco companies killed Frank Lartigue "not by running over him with one of their trucks, but causing his death just as effectively by the use of products manufactured and sold by them." Displaying packages of King Bee tobacco and Picayune cigarettes (products of Liggett & Myers) and a package of Camels (produced by Reynolds), he said Frank Lartigue was "a cigarette fiend" who smoked a cigarette the first thing in the morning and all through the day "and smoked every cigarette down to the butt." After telling the story of Lartigue's hospitalization for cancer of the vocal cords and lung cancer, he said the plaintiff would show that Liggett & Myers and Reynolds

> had a responsibility, a duty, to make their products wholesome, to make their product in such a manner that it wouldn't kill people or cause them harm . . . that there was a breach and a violation of that chargeable responsibility, not only was it so unwholesome that it made Mr. Lartigue ill, it gave him the cancer of the throat . . . that these products, Camel cigarettes, Picayune cigarettes and King Bee tobacco have cancer producing substances in them. As he smoked he inhaled cancer producing substances . . . condensate known as tar. [The two companies] never gave any warning of any kind . . . that these products were unwholesome.

On the contrary, Brumfield said, the ads of the cigarette manufacturers "extoll their virtues and said how wholesome they really were and that they were not harmful." Just a generation ago lung cancer was a rare disease, "unknown practically," the lawyer for the plaintiff continued, and added that today lung cancer is the most common cause of death in man of any cancer in any site in his body. Over the past twenty years, he said, evidence would show that death from lung cancer has multiplied ten times—"that the more you smoke the more your chances are that you will die of lung cancer, and as you decrease in your smoking, lung cancer will decrease your probability of getting this dread disease." He then asked damages of $150,000 for Mrs. Lartigue, a considerable reduction from the original claim of $779,500.

The defense then took the stand. In his opening statement for R. J. Reynolds, attorney Theodore Kiendl described Frank Lartigue as a very unhealthy man who had many diseases in his early life and was "a prospect for most any type of disease." Kiendl said Lartigue smoked to an "absurd excess," never stopped smoking, and, in fact, his wife had testified in a pretrial deposition that his smoking was so bad that she "had to get out of the house lots of times." Furthermore, he said, referring to the description by the plaintiff's lawyer, Lartigue was a "cigarette fiend" as early as 1899, when he was only nine years old. This was surely contributory negligence, he argued. Kiendl told the jury that there was no basis for monetary recovery based on anything that happened after July, 1955, the time of Lartigue's death. "Prior to that time medical science had not reached the point where it could be said that smoking cigarettes could cause this condition," he argued. "The cause of cancer today, as many doctors testify, is still as much of a mystery as ever." Kiendl sharply criticized the plaintiff's attorney for requesting the jury to bring in a verdict for the widow in the sum of $150,000, pointing out that the amount sought in the original suit was $779,500. But even the lesser amount was "a dream," he said, asserting that he would produce evidence to show that while Lartigue was still alive he asked R. J. Reynolds for $750 for hospitalization expenses and $750 for loss of work due to his illness. "We take the flat-footed position that there is no liability here whatsoever."

Harry Kelleher of the New Orleans law firm of Lemle and Kelleher, representing Liggett & Myers, told the jury he adopted Kiendl's opening statement. But he reminded them that his firm had not been established until 1911, ten years after Lartigue started smoking. He pointed out that, until 1911, King Bee tobacco and Picayune cigarettes had been manufactured by the W. R. Irby Company of New Orleans. (Reynolds and Liggett & Myers both emerged from the dissolution of the old American Tobacco Company following government antitrust action against the tobacco trust, as did American and Lorillard.)

On the third day of trial, September 21, the parade of expert witnesses began. Dr. B. L. Van Duuren, research chemist at New York University Medical School, told the jury that "carcinogenic material" is found in all forms of tobacco smoke and produces cancer in animals. The witness said he had worked with biologists and saw the results of experiments in which some of these cancer-inducing substances were painted on the backs of mice. "I saw what the biologists call tumors," he said. "I saw growths—sores." These assertions prompted strong objections from defense attorneys, who cited an earlier cancer-cigarette case (the *Green* case in Florida) in which the judge had ruled out references to animal experiments. "We do not know whether man is more or less susceptible than mice to particular carcinogens," said Kiendl. He added that animals also differ in this regard, noting that none of the most powerful carcinogens had been shown to produce tumors in monkeys. To admit testimony on animal experiments would "take us out into the wild blue yonder . . . open the door for prejudicial material."

Plaintiff's attorney Belli responded that that door had been opened by Pasteur. "We can show that tar from chimneys painted on mouse ears will give cancer and in one instance we can show that the same type of soot or tar painted on the scrotum of the chimney sweep will give the same type of cancer."

Picking up this indirect reference to the well-known high incidence of cancer among chimney sweeps in Great Britain, the defense lawyer said: "There has never been one reported case where the chimney sweep who inhaled the same tars had cancer of the scrotum." Addressing Judge Christenberry, he complained, "I think we are opening a Pandora's box, your honor." A prolonged discussion then ensued in the absence of the jury. Judge Christenberry ruled finally that he would admit testimony on the results of animal-cancer studies made since 1957. He cautioned the jury later to keep in mind that these materials might well have different effects on humans.

Animal experiments were the subject of testimony right up to the last day of trial. Dr. Ernest L. Wynder, whose experiments with mice in the early 1950's sparked the controversy, did not appear to testify in person. But he did give a deposition in New York, where he was then on the staff of the Sloan-Kettering Institute and chief of the epidemiology section of the New York Memorial cancer hospital. Epidemiology is a fairly new study that attempts to find out why different diseases occur in various population groups at different rates. Dr. Wynder testified that cigarette-smoke condensates placed on the skin of mice and rabbits produce cancer in a certain percentage of cases. "I will say today that the total information and all the answers to the cancer problem, of course, are still a puzzle to man," he added. "We believe that we have ruled in several other factors besides smoking, though we have always stated that smoking was the most important cause. We have always stated that there must be the element of predisposition, because obviously not every smoker develops cancer. But we have always stated that smoking was the major factor."

Dr. Alton Ochsner had already been described to the jury as a "genius" in the field of thoracic surgery who had treated more cancer patients than any other man alive. When the gray-haired, dignified surgeon took the stand, it was the first time he had testified before a jury on lung cancer. During the hour consumed in questioning Dr. Ochsner on his qualifications, it was brought out that he had personally seen about 2,000 lung-cancer patients and had operated on about half that number. The other half, he said, were cases that had advanced to the point where nothing could be done for the patient by operating. Of the patients he had seen, the doctor said that about 85 per cent had squamous-cell cancers caused by cigarette-smoking. The other 12 to 15 per cent had cancers of another type that he did not attribute to smoking. Asked how many of the 2,000 lung-cancer patients were alive after five years, the physician replied: "The number is pitifully low. There is only a 5 per cent survival rate." Of those operated on, about 15 per cent were still alive after five years. The doctor recommended that everyone who smokes have a lung X-ray every three months.

Dr. Ochsner said that he had first become interested in the lung-cancer question in the 1930's and had made a presentation to the Clinical Congress of the American College of Surgeons in 1938, in which he said that "the increase in smoking with the universal custom of inhaling is probably a responsible factor in the case of lung cancer."

Since then, he testified that more than 400 of his scientific papers had been published, about fifty of them dealing with lung cancer. Dr. Ochsner was also the author of a popular book on the subject of smoking: *Smoking and Your Life* (New York: Simon and Schuster, 1964) .

There was a period between 1946 and 1948 when certain studies were made that indicated that there was no causal relationship between cancer and smoking, the surgeon testified. But in 1949, he said, it was found that hospital records regarding the smoking records of patients were incorrect. "If we asked a patient if he smoked he would say 'no,' and we would find out that he had stopped the day before. We learned that we had to have scientific smoking records. People suspected of having cancer apparently were ashamed of their smoking." A special smoking history form was later devised for cancer patients.

Dr. Ochsner testified that in 1959, the year prior to the trial, some 30,000 to 40,000 persons had died of lung cancer and that 85 per cent of these deaths were due to smoking. In 1934, there was a tremendous increase in the incidence of bronchogenic cancer in men, he said, because twenty years before, at the beginning of World War I, men began to smoke cigarettes heavily. The twenty-year lag was just about the right length of time for the cancer-producing effect of tobacco to exert itself, the witness said. "It is the ones that began twenty years ago that determines the ones that are going to develop cancer." The surgeon also read from a paper he delivered to the 1951 annual meeting of the American Medical Association, in which he predicted that cancer caused by smoking would become the most common form of lung cancer. "It is frightening to speculate on the possible number of bronchogenic cancers that may develop because of the tremendous numbers of cigarettes consumed in the two decades from 1930 to 1950."

As to Frank Lartigue, Dr. Ochsner testified that he had examined the autopsy report and concluded that the husband of the plaintiff died of epidermoid cancer caused by smoking. On cross-examination, Kiendl asked, "It doesn't matter what all of the other facts were, if the two cardinal factors, smoking and cancer, were there, your answer would be the same, all of the other facts would be surpluses?"

"Yes."

"Is it fair to state that you have a profound aversion to smoking?"

"No, I am frightened," the surgeon replied. "I have no aversion to smoking. As a physician I am frightened as to what it does."

The defense counsel also questioned the New Orleans physician on the reported predisposition of men to lung cancer, reminding him that in a 1948 article in *Southern Surgeons,* Dr. Ochsner had written:

> The etiology of bronchogenic carcinoma is unknown, aside from the fact that males are much more frequently involved than females. . . . On the other hand, one cannot say what is the cause, what the cause is of increasing incidence of this type of malignant disease, malignant process. Although we previously were of the opinion that chronic irritation resulting from excessive cigarette smoking was a factor, this cannot be proved.

Dr. Ochsner said that he changed his mind on the question of sexual predisposition as research advanced. "I have seen some persons develop cancer of the lung after six years of smoking, some after many years. Generally a pack a day for twenty or twenty-five years in the male is the time needed to produce a malignancy."

Mrs. Lartigue took the witness stand on Wednesday morning, September 29, to tell the court that her husband was "a slave to his cigarettes." During all their married life, she said, her husband smoked about two packs a day of Picayune cigarettes and rolled that amount from King Bee tobacco. "Many is the time I begged him not to smoke," she said. "He couldn't do without them." She also testified that while Lartigue was in the army during World War I he suffered from shortness of breath and could not drill. "He developed a bad cough which he had for twenty-five or thirty years before his death," she told the court. "Three years before his operation in 1954 for cancer of the throat he became very hoarse," she said. Lartigue was operated on at Ochsner Foundation Hospital in 1954 and his vocal cords were removed.

As the trial went into its second week, the plaintiff continued to bring a parade of expert witnesses to the stand, some of whom claimed that the "tars" from burning tobacco contain chemical irritants which produce lung cancer. But R. J. Reynolds's vice president in charge of manufacturing, Haddon S. Kirk, said in a deposition that the tobacco industry never used the word "tar." Kirk said his firm had reports for many years showing the nicotine content of its cigarettes, but nothing about tars. In about 1952, he said, the firm became interested in the relation between smoking and lung cancer, and the Tobacco Industry Research Committee was formed. The TIRC never reported anything deleterious in tobacco, Kirk said. He also claimed that large-scale promotion of filter-tip cigarettes had nothing to do with any alleged connection between smoking and lung cancer.

William Augustus Blount, vice president in charge of manufacturing and processing for Liggett & Myers, said no tests had been made for tars on either King Bee or Picayunes. In a deposition, he told the plaintiff's attorneys, "I don't know what you're talking about," when they inquired about tar content. Blount said Liggett & Myers did not belong to the TIRC, that its own research facilities were better and faster. He referred throughout his deposition to "smoking residue" and said that people had known for hundreds of years that black oils come from the smoke. "It will take another twenty-five to thirty years to tell what is in these oils."

On Friday, October 1, defense attorneys called their first witness, Dr. Thomas H. Burford, professor of surgery at Washington University in St. Louis. Dr. Burford had trained under Dr. Evarts Graham, the man who had performed the first total removal of the lung, in the 1930's, when thoracic surgery was born. In 1952, Dr. Burford succeeded his superior as chief of thoracic surgery at Barnes Hospital in St. Louis. Dr. Burford said he had attended more than 2,000 cancer cases and had operated on more than 1,275 "from all walks of life, all social and economic strata, all occupations and all races." Asked by defense attorney Harry Kelleher if he had an opinion on the incidence of lung cancer among nonsmokers, he said: "It definitely does occur. In my own opinion it has appeared in between 20 and 25 per cent of the cases."

The following exchange then took place between the defense attorney and Dr. Burford:

Q. Doctor, at my request have you examined the clinical record on Frank J. Lartigue?
A. I have.
Q. From Ochsner Foundation Hospital?
A. I have.
Q. Have you also examined the clinical records on Frank J. Lartigue from the Veterans Administration Hospital where he had his terminal illness?
A. I have.

Q. Have you also examined at my request his army medical record?

A. Yes, sir.

Q. Now, Doctor, can you say with reasonable medical certainty that cigarette smoking is *the* cause of epidermoid lung cancer?

A. No.

Q. Can you say with reasonable medical certainty that cigarette-smoking is *a* cause of epidermoid lung cancer?

A. No.

Q. Can you say with reasonable medical certainty that it is *probable* that cigarette-smoking is the cause of epidermoid lung cancer?

A. I cannot.

Q. Can you say with reasonable medical certainty that smoking is a contributing cause of such epidermoid lung cancer?

A. No.

Q. Is it a generally accepted medical fact in the medical community that cigarette-smoking is a cause of epidermoid lung cancer?

A. No, it is not.

Q. Would your answers to the questions I have just submitted to you be the same with regard to other forms of lung cancer?

A. They would.

Q. Now, Doctor, I propose to submit a hypothetical question to you, and for the purpose of that question, I should like you to assume the facts which I shall now state to be true facts:

Frank J. Lartigue died July 13, 1955, at the age of sixty-five.

He smoked at least two packs of cigarettes per day for a period of forty-one years from 1913 until his death in

1954, and he commenced smoking when he was nine years old.

Lartigue was in the army in World War I for a period of approximately six months. He traveled continuously on various jobs in connection with his work from the time he was discharged from the army until he had an operation for laryngofissure in October of 1954 at Ochsner Foundation Hospital in New Orleans.

Since the early 1930's, this traveling was continuous and was by automobile, and some of it was on black-top roads.

Mr. Lartigue was a short man, approximately 5 feet, 4 inches or so in height and weighed 120 to 125 pounds.

In childhood he had measles, diphtheria, whooping cough, chronic tonsillitis, and swelling of the feet and ankles. He had amblyopia accommodative, which is dimness of vision in the left eye.

He had gonorrhea in 1910, with bubo and enlargement of the lymphatic gland in the groin, which was operated on in 1911.

While in the army, he was hospitalized as follows. From July 7, 1918, with tertiary syphilis, which existed before he went into the army. He was poorly nourished, and from September 27, 1918, to October 5th he was hospitalized for influenza.

From November 11th to November 20th, he was hospitalized wtih chronic anterior and posterior gonorrheal urethritis, syphilis manifested by penile chancre, and acute enteritis.

While in the army, he had a rundown condition and was weak and too short-breathed to drill and had a dry cough. He had malaria in 1914 and 1916. He had a cough continuing from about the time he was in the army until he died. He had rheumatic pains, which, together with his cough, forced him to give up his insurance business in 1934.

All of his teeth were extracted either just after he left the army in 1919 or perhaps as late as 1932.

X-ray reports reveal calcified deposits bilaterally. The autopsy protocol from the Veterans Administration Hospital in Houston, Texas, where he had his terminal illness, revealed a small calcified nodule in the upper left lobe anteriorly.

The autopsy protocol also revealed in the section relating to the microscopic examination of the lung, that in the tunica propria and muscularis mucosae are numerous lymphocytes, plasma cells, large mononuclear cells, and neutrophilic granulocytes.

He had a laryngofissure for cancer of the larynx on October 5, 1954, but no X-ray was taken nor was any X-ray taken at postoperative examination on November 15 and December 30, 1954.

As of December 2, 1954, Lartigue's swollen neck and face and flamed eyes, blueness of chest, and pains in the back of his neck and shoulders prevented his sleeping at night.

On December 30, 1954, an X-ray was requested, and X-rays were taken at Ochsner Foundation Hospital on February 14th and 24th, and lung cancer was discovered at that time.

Lartigue died on July 13, 1955, the cause of his death being cancer of the lung.

Now, Doctor, assuming the correctness of the facts I have stated to you in the hypothetical question, can you say with medical certainty whether or not Frank H. Lartigue's lung cancer was caused by prolonged or excessive cigarette-smoking?

A. No, I cannot.

My opinion is cigarette-smoking does not cause cancer of the lung. I base this opinion upon my clinical experience and upon my observations.

Dr. Evarts Graham and I, I presume, have as large a collective experience in cancer of the lung as any two surgeons in the world, and in that collective experience, we saw only two—I mean four—cancers of the structure called the trachea.

Now, the trachea, and very probably this has been brought out here before, has the same type of epithelial lining that the major windpipes do. This structure gets the blast of cigarette smoke coming and going, and yet, as I have said, in our large experience we only saw four cases of cancer of the trachea.

I have already testified that in my group I have seen between 20 per cent and 25 per cent of people who have had epidermoid carcinoma who have never smoked anything. There is the well-known difference between the male and the female, and in our particular group, this differential between the male and the female is not narrowing, it is in our group remaining the same or perhaps widening a bit. That is to say, the male still has five times the amount of lung cancer that the female does.

In our experience—and I take into consideration, too, the very large number of heavy smokers who never develop a lung cancer—I am mindful in my own experience of the striking incidence one sees rather frequently where one will encounter a number of very old males in a family, none of whom have ever had a cancer. Contrarywise, there are those families that are relatively shot through with cancer.

In a larger, more philosophical sense, I as a surgeon am impressed by the fact that cancer of the colon or bowel, cancer in the stomach, cancer in the lung, or cancer in the breast are all of the same piece. It is a terrific biologic phenomenon. It is not understood. No man knows the cause of lung cancer. Certainly, not I. Certainly no group that any doctor or any scientist knows can as of this date give the answer to this very important and very fundamental question.

If that question were answered, I would not be here today, sir.

The taking of testimony in the long cigarette-cancer trial was concluded on Friday, October 8. Some twelve doctors and scientists, about one-half of the total testifying for both sides, shared Dr. Burford's opinion and so testified. Oral arguments to the jury were due to begin at 10 A.M. Monday. Attorneys for the plaintiff rested after two rebuttal witnesses were heard. Judge Christenberry took under advisement motions for a directed verdict presented by attorneys for both sides. On Monday, jurors listened to six hours of final arguments by opposing counsel. H. Alva Brumfield and Melvin M. Belli, allotted three hours for their side of the argument, pointed out to the jury that their verdict must be by a preponderance of the evidence rather than on proof beyond a reasonable doubt as required in criminal cases. "The evidence must tilt the scale a little bit in her favor, but there can be some doubt," Brumfield said. He accused the tobacco companies of "brainwashing" and of "taking no steps to warn the public of the harmful effects of their products." During his presentation, he used pages of the official trial transcript enlarged so that the jury could read along with him as he reviewed the testimony.

The opening argument for the defense was presented by Theodore Kiendl, who told the jury that the only issues remaining in the case after three weeks of trial were the issues of implied warranty, negligence of the defendants, the question of contributory negligence on the part of Lartigue, and the question of damages. Kiendl reviewed Lartigue's history of smoking two packages of cigarettes a day, but he argued that the plaintiff's husband probably smoked nearer to five packs a day. The medical evidence in the case, the lawyer argued, showed that there was no general acceptance in the medical profession of the idea that there is a causal relationship between lung cancer and cigarette-smoking. The evidence produced by the tobacco companies shows that nonsmokers get lung cancers, that the overwhelming number of smokers do not get lung cancer, and that the increase in the incidence of lung cancer is apparent rather than real. Kiendl described lung cancer as a disease associated with old age and with the deterioration of the body tissues and cells. But in any event, defense counsel said that Liggett & Myers and R. J. Reynolds had nothing to do with starting Lartigue on his smoking career and that the plaintiff had made "extravagant and exaggerated claims" and tried to "capitalize on the death of her husband." He argued that Lartigue smoked "to an absurd excess . . . as much as anyone you have ever heard of in the world." The lawyer asserted that Mrs. Lartigue was "not entitled to a single dollar."

In an hour-long charge to the jury, Judge Christenberry said the action was based on both charges of negligence and breach of warranty. "As a fundamental principle of law, before any person can be charged with negligence of this sort, it must be established that he had knowledge of some inherent danger or defective condition of his product," the judge told the jury, and continued:

This knowledge may be either actual knowledge or such knowledge as a reasonably prudent man should have acquired under the circumstances. Plaintiff must prove that defendants knew or should have known before Mr. Lartigue's lung cancer started, that their product could cause that disease. Under the circumstances of this case, such knowledge can only be had by these defendants if medical science also had it and had made it publicly known at the time that Mr. Lartigue's lung cancer started. The mere failure to warn against the result, which could not have been reasonably anticipated, is not actionable negligence. The defendants cannot be held guilty of negligence on the basis of medical opinion, surveys, or other similar materials not announced until after that time.

Judge Christenberry had denied a plea by the plaintiff's attorneys that the jury be given a list of specific questions to answer as part of their verdict. The questions concerned the alleged negligence of the tobacco companies, the causal relationship of smoking and lung cancer, and other issues. He submitted the case to the jury on a general verdict form, on which the jurors could record a verdict for the plaintiff against one or both of the defendants with the amount of the damages, or a verdict for the two tobacco companies. The jury was also told by the judge that the plaintiff must have proved her case by a preponderance of evidence and not beyond a reasonable doubt as in a criminal case.

At 11:05 A.M., on October 11, the jury took the case under advisement. At 12:45 P.M., after deliberating for one hour and forty minutes, the jury returned to the courtroom with a general verdict for the tobacco companies. The seventeen-day trial produced twenty volumes of testimony, not to speak of exhibits, most of it devoted to medical opinion. The jury had the benefit of chemical studies, epidemiological studies, reports of animal experiments, pathological evidence, reports of clinical observations, and the testimony of renowned doctors.

The only hint as to the jury's reasoning came in some later remarks of Judge Christenberry in the course of a hearing on the plaintiff's unsuccessful motion for a new trial. He then said: "I regret now I did not propound the interrogatory with respect to the connection between the smoking and his lung cancer, because I'm satisfied the jury never got beyond that question and I know— I'm sure, at least—that they simply decided the plaintiff had failed to prove the causal connection between his smoking and his lung cancer. But that is water under the bridge now."

✦ 8

The Surgeon General's Bomb

THERE HAVE BEEN TIMES IN HISTORY when the work of one man has changed the course of an industry. Upton Sinclair in the early part of the century brought the attention of an outraged public to the stench of Chicago meatpacking. Ralph Nader, with his book *Unsafe at Any Speed* (New York: Grossman, 1965), single-handedly rocked the automobile industry. Frances Kelsey, a doctor on the staff of the U.S. Food and Drug Administration (FDA), shocked the world and especially the pharmaceutical barons with her revelations that the drug thalidomide, when taken by pregnant women, could produce hideous deformities in babies.

Because of the consumer legislation passed, the 1960's have been called the Decade of the Consumer. But despite isolated instances, the problem of organizing mass support to bring about change in consumer-protection laws has remained. As for bringing a particular issue to the top of the government's agenda, there are no guides, no instruction manuals. It takes careful, intelligent planning, much hard work, and a lot of luck. Consumer forces have to put together large coalitions of marginal interest groups to capture the public imagination. Resistance to change is built into what social scientists refer to as special-interest subsystems.

The question of what should be done to inform the public about the medical evidence against smoking had been kicking around one government agency or another in Washington for almost forty years. But there had been bickering among the federal agencies themselves. The Federal Trade Commission did not see how it could require a warning without a definite government policy on the health issue. The Department of Health, Education, and Welfare (HEW), parent of the FDA and the Public Health Service, was generally unenthusiastic about taking on the tobacco industry, although the PHS had undertaken research and shown some interest in action. The FDA had been given a chance to concern itself with cigarette-smoking when the Hazardous Substances Labeling Act was passed in 1960. That law empowered the agency, among other things, to control the sale of substances with the capacity to induce illness through inhalation. But HEW appeared to be uncertain about whether the law covered cigarettes. Anthony Celebrezze, who followed Abraham A. Ribicoff as President John F. Kennedy's Secretary of HEW, later asked Congress for a clarification on that point. But until the tobacco subsystem began to quake, the department avoided controversy by doing nothing.

The Department of Agriculture was something else again. Ever since Jamestowners rushed to duplicate John Rolfe's garden in the seventeenth century, responsible officials had been puzzled by leaf surpluses and how to maintain certain market averages for the product. As early as 1924, a bill was proposed in Congress to set up an export corporation with government funds to buy surplus leaf on the domestic market to sell abroad. The idea was defeated four times before the Depression of 1930 changed men's minds. In the flurry of New Deal legislation, tobacco was not overlooked. It was one of the basic commodities covered by the Agricultural Adjustment Act of 1933. The "adjustment" took the form of acreage restrictions and loans against surplus production. When the national economy went into another decline five years later, a second control was added. Marketing quotas, which were actually acreage limits, were set subject to a vote by two-thirds of the farmers themselves. Pools were established to receive leaf from farmers who received cash on the hogshead. This operation was underwritten by loans from the government. From 1938 on, price records were set for flue-cured (Bright) and Burley. In that year, next to grain, tobacco was the most valuable farm crop grown in North America. Demand might push the price up, as in 1956–57, when Burley averaged 63.3 cents a pound. "Parity payment" loans prevented the price from collapsing; a farmer with gradable tobacco could turn it over to the government for a price equal to 90 per cent of parity—a price designed to keep purchasing power constant. The parity formula was computed by the Department of Agriculture. Price supports encouraged quantity production, sometimes at the expense of quality.

By 1956, there were 200 million pounds of leaf in the government-financed pool. Officials at the Department of Agriculture wielded power over an enormous investment of the taxpayer's money. They naturally took a somewhat proprietary proindustry position in the health matter, which they preferred to ignore. The department was actively engaged in promoting sales of tobacco both at home and abroad. It was distributing an expensive sales promotion film showing the virtues of smoking. The film was available free of charge to any nation that might want to consider importing U.S. tobacco products.

A federal tax had been placed on some tobacco products in 1794. James Madison opposed a levy on all tobacco commodities, arguing before Congress that "The pleasures of life consisted in a series of innocent gratifications," among which was the social use of tobacco. The excise was applied first only to snuff, and in 1796 even that was repealed. Following the War of 1812, a "war-cost" tax was imposed on all manufactured tobacco, but that, too, was repealed after only ten months. The federal government's need for revenue during the Civil War brought an internal revenue tax on most tobacco commodities. By 1962, the federal tax on tobacco products had been in effect for exactly 100 years, and at 8 cents a pack, it was ten times the original levy. Iowa was the first state to adopt a tobacco tax. Since 1921, when the Iowa law went into effect, the states had collected $10 billion in tobacco taxes.

Retail trade in tobacco commodities had long been an important source of government revenue, most of it paid by the nearly 70 million cigarette-smokers. Taxes took about 48 per cent of every dollar consumers paid for cigarettes, or about 43 per cent of the retail cost of all tobacco products. This tax money went to federal, state, county, and municipal treasuries. In calendar year 1962, the tax on manufactured tobacco brought $2,030,304,000 to the U.S. Treasury, an amount that gave it third place in internal-revenue collections from commodities. (The federal excise on tobacco products goes into general Treasury funds. State and municipal treasuries allocate tobacco-tax income for educational and health needs, public welfare, recreational facilities, and the like.) In 1962, cigarette taxes provided the states with $1,129,879,000, and the counties and municipalities with more than $50 million.

Tobacco had become a powerful force in American politics. The tobacco coalition included not only the industry itself but a clientele of millions of people who annually smoked about 494.5 billion cigarettes and other tobacco products worth nearly $8 billion. The recipients of that money included manufacturers, ad agencies, the mass media, farmers, shopkeepers, and tax collectors. By 1962, tobacco ranked fourth in the over-all value of cash crops grown by American farmers. In that year, it brought farmers $1.3 billion. In 1962, leaf exports were worth $374 million, putting tobacco third in the dollar value of agricultural exports. In addition, more than $220 million worth of cigarettes and other tobacco commodities were exported. Some 750,000 American farm families were engaged in tobacco production, and at the height of the growing and harvesting seasons some 3 million workers were employed in different phases of the agriculture. The general pattern of distribution was to deposit the packaged goods in warehouses that served as depots for all manufacturers. These warehouses were located in the most active marketing centers of the United States. For them, delivery was made to some 5,000 wholesalers. The wholesalers distributed tobacco merchandise to about 700,000 retail stores, including independent food stores, supermarket chains, drug stores, restaurants, other outlets, and the servicers of more than 800,000 vending machines. (Cigarettes had become the most accessible of all consumer products.) The four leading states in terms of both production and relative dependence on the crop were North Carolina, Kentucky, South Carolina, and Virginia. In seven states, tobacco receipts exceeded 10 per cent of total cash receipts from all commodities. Attempts to discourage smoking would therefore affect the lives of millions of people with profound economic and political consequences.

The tobacco subsystem had succeeded in keeping the health question a low-priority item on the government's agenda by playing one government agency off against another. Tobacco policy was controlled in a cooperative spirit by a coalition of certain segments of Congress, the bureaucracy, and industry. Like hundreds of others in Washington, the tobacco subsystem cut across institutional lines and included the paid representatives of tobacco-growers, marketing organizations, and manufacturers. The tobacco leaf was woven so deeply into the fabric of American life that it was used as a motif in the decoration of columns in the Capitol. Congressmen representing tobacco-growing states were leading members of four subcommittees, including two appropriations subcommittees and two committees in each house of Congress handling tobacco legislation. All of these people in the agencies and in Congress knew each other well, and, as long as there was no public outcry, certain programs, such as tobacco price supports and export promotion, were carried on without interference.

Tobacco power was thus firmly entrenched and well supported. Each medical discovery and government response had been met by a reaction from the manufacturers and their advertisers. The tobacco subsystem appeared impenetrable to the demands of the antismoking forces.

In 1961, the Tobacco Institute staged a celebration of the 350th anniversary of America's first tobacco crop. The festival, complete with a cigar-smoking John Rolfe and an alluring Pocahontas, was well publicized. In addition to distributing copies of a magnificently illustrated historical treatise entitled *Tobacco & Americans* (New York:

McGraw-Hill, 1960), by Robert K. Heimann, a one-time journalist and social scientist who had become a high official of the American Tobacco Company, the Institute distributed kits to enable young scientists to grow their own tobacco varieties from seed. The Institute, with its public relations firm, Hill and Knowlton, was sending to more than a hundred thousand physicians around the country a quarterly publication called *Tobacco and Health Research,* a summary and compendium of items having to do with research on these subjects, under such headings as "Autopsy Study Fails to Support Smoking Tie to Vascular Ills," "Lung Cancer Deaths 20% Overstated," and "Miners' Lung Cancers Triple Average."

In June, 1962, the Institute issued a statement declaring that the tobacco industry had always taken the position that "smoking is a custom for adults," and that, in conformity with this belief, a number of companies had decided to discontinue advertising in college publications and engaging in other campus promotional activities. For years, most companies had been conducting campaigns to persuade college students to smoke their particular brands, both through placing advertising in college publications (the cigarette industry became the biggest single source of revenue for many such publications) and through the promotional activities of paid "campus representatives," who gave away sample packs. The Institute's declaration that smoking was a "custom for adults" had one result that applied more broadly.

In the fall of 1962, the American Tobacco Company began an extensive campaign for Lucky Strike in which the advertising copy contained the statement that "smoking is a pleasure meant for adults." This sentiment was expressed under a headline, spread over two pages, "Lucky Strike Separates the Men from the Boys . . . but Not from the Girls." Shown on one side of the page was a helmeted racing-car driver flourishing a winner's cup as admiring youths gathered around. On the other side of the page, the same winning driver was being hugged by his girl friend. Smoking Lucky Strike was apparently the trick that turned a boy into a man.

The industry-supported Tobacco Industry Research Committee was sticking to its position that the relationship between smoking and health had not been sufficiently investigated, that it remained to be seen whether genetic, hormonal, emotional, and other differences between smokers and nonsmokers, as well as differences in their external environment, afford clues to their differing health risks, and that the cause of cancer, as such, was still unknown. In 1957, before Representative John A. Blatnik's subcommittee of the Government Operations Committee, Dr. Ernest L. Wynder of the famed Sloan-Kettering Institute of Cancer Research had said:

> I am all in favor of the tobacco industry supporting research in this country. If they spent $2 million to further research in cancer or the tobacco-cancer problem, it is all so much the better. But I was a little discouraged if after two and a half years Dr. Clarence Cook Little publishes his first report, after spending perhaps $2 million, and reported that they found very little. I am sure that the director of my institute, after I had spent that much money on research and after two and a half years, and I had to report I found practically nothing, would be a little bit unhappy.

While some experts both at home and abroad agreed with TIRC's Dr. Little, various governments had taken steps to discourage smoking, especially among young people. The Ministry of Health in Britain, where the lung-cancer death rate was even higher than the United States, acted on the recommendation of the Royal College of Physicians and adopted a program of publicity to warn people that cigarette-smoking is dangerous to health. A million or so posters had been distributed to schools, post offices, and other public buildings, with such inscriptions as: "Before You Smoke, Think: Cigarettes Cause Lung Cancer." The Independent Television Authority in England, the group that governs commercial television, had come to an agreement with British cigarette-manufacturers to limit the showing of cigarette commercials to the hours after 9 P.M., when children would be in bed. An elaborate set of rules had also been adopted to govern advertising on TV. West Germany and Denmark had taken certain measures to restrict cigarette advertising. And the Soviet Union, where tobacco is a state monopoly, had taken the somewhat contradictory step of mounting a poster campaign against cigarette-smoking.

In the United States, there had been no official action. There had been warnings from many quarters, including the Commissioner of Health for New York State and a World Health Organization study group. Then, gradually, the ball began to roll. In 1961, the heads of the prominent voluntary health organizations, the American Cancer Society, the American Public Health Association, the American Heart Association, and the National Tuberculosis Association, urged the President to establish a commission to study the "widespread implications of the tobacco problem." On January 4, 1962, representatives of the four organizations met with Surgeon General Luther L. Terry. Shortly thereafter, in March, 1962, Senator Maurine Neuberger introduced a Senate Resolution calling for establishment of a Presidential commission on tobacco and health. The senator knew from experience that Congress would ignore the issue. She had merely wanted to provide a vehicle for action.

Senator Neuberger's resolution lay dormant for two months. Then one day a reporter at one of President Kennedy's news conferences asked him what he intended to do about the question of smoking and health. The President, known for his wit and confidence in handling these get-togethers with the press, was evidently caught unprepared. With some hesitation, obvious in the transcript of the exchange, he replied: "That matter is sensitive enough and the stock market is in sufficient difficulty without my giving you an answer which is not based on complete information, which I don't have, and, therefore, perhaps I would be glad to respond to that question in more detail next week."

The White House accordingly asked the Public Health Service what it was doing about the smoking-health question. The studies that had been made within PHS since 1957 provided the basis for a rapid response. Just two weeks after the President's request, Surgeon General Terry announced that he would set up a blue-ribbon advisory committee to "assess available knowledge in this area and make appropriate recommendations." This action was approved by President Kennedy the same day. Actually, this wasn't the sort of Presidential commission Senator Neuberger had had in mind. But her resolution had provided the spark needed to move the bureaucracy to display its latent policy-making powers.

In April, Senator Neuberger had written to the FTC's newly appointed chairman, Paul Rand Dixon, who had served as general counsel to the Kefauver antimonopoly subcommittee, which had a lot to say about drug prices. Senator Neuberger suggested that any cigarette ad that did not carry a health warning should be found deceptive.

Why, she asked, couldn't the FTC require that all cigarette advertising carry a health warning? In response to her letter, Chairman Dixon said that if the commission was "able to secure competent probative scientific evidence including that furnished by the Public Health Service, that a causal relationship exists between cigarette smoking and lung cancer, heart ailments, etc., it is likely that an order of the Commission, based on such evidence . . . would be upheld in the appellate courts." About the time the Surgeon General set up his advisory committee, the FTC announced adoption of general rule-making procedures that would enable it to impose such a requirement on an industry-wide basis. A medical doctor on the staff of the FTC participated in the initial deliberations of the Surgeon General's Advisory Committee. Months before completion of its report, the commission had organized a task force consisting of lawyers, physicians, and economists to review and make recommendations with respect to its responsibilities in the area of cigarette advertising and labeling.

The Surgeon General's Advisory Committee was chosen with the politics of policy-making clearly in mind. The report of such a high-level committee would have a significant impact on the public, and, it was hoped, would give the Public Health Service the support it needed to pursue a program to reduce the health threat posed by mass cigarette consumption. The committee was given a mandate, not to make a new scientific study of its own but to review the existing evidence.

That the Surgeon General intended to influence public opinion could be seen in the way the ten members were chosen. The group was to include scientific and professional people concerned with all aspects of smoking and health. The Surgeon General called on the tobacco industry, health groups, the federal agencies, and professional associations to participate in selecting from a list of 150 scientists. These groups could eliminate anyone they did not want. One blackball could eliminate any name. This device was designed to avoid any accusation that the committee had been, in any way, stacked. Anyone who had made public statements on the smoking-health issue was automatically eliminated. As finally selected, the committee was composed of M.D.'s with such specialties as internal medicine, epidemiology, and pharmacology, including professors at leading medical schools, a chemist, and a statistician. Three of them smoked cigarettes and two smoked pipes or cigars. Dr. Terry acted as chairman and Dr. James M. Hundley, assistant surgeon general, as vice chairman. The members, announced on October 27, 1962, were: Dr. Stanhope Bayne-Jones, former dean, Yale School of Medicine; Dr. Walter J. Burdette, head of the Department of Surgery, University of Utah School of Medicine; William G. Cochran, professor of Statistics, Harvard University; Dr. Emmanuel Farber, chairman, Department of Pathology, University of Pittsburgh; Louis F. Fieser, professor of Organic Chemistry, Harvard University; Dr. Jacob Furth, professor of Pathology, Columbia University; Dr. John B. Hickam, chairman, Department of Internal Medicine, Indiana University; Dr. Charles LeMaistre, professor of Internal Medicine, the University of Texas Southwestern Medical School; Dr. Leonard M. Schuman, professor of Epidemiology, University of Minnesota School of Public Health; Dr. Maurice H. Seevers, chairman, Department of Pharmacology, University of Michigan.

The members were paid consultant fees and began their work shortly after the announcement was made. In tackling the monumental task of reviewing the scientific literature, the group had the services of many consultants, half-a-dozen professional staff members, plus secretarial and technical aid. During 1963, the full committee held nine meetings of from two to four days' duration. Extraordinary precautions were taken to maintain secrecy, and the Washington press corps speculated fruitlessly about what was taking place inside the Public Health Service's headquarters in suburban Bethesda, Maryland. Strict security was maintained to avoid the spreading of erroneous information. What little information did leak out provided no comfort to the tobacco industry.

There was one surprise reaction to all this. Shortly after the advisory committee began to work, Leroy Collins, president of the National Association of Broadcasters (NAB), called on his industry, the recipient of the lion's share of cigarette advertising, to take "corrective action" against the televising of certain kinds of commercials directed at children. The NAB president, a former Democratic governor of Florida, said broadcasters had a moral responsibility not to "ignore the mounting evidence that tobacco provides a serious hazard to health." Speaking to the fall conference of NAB members at Portland, Oregon, Collins said the most recent statistics he had seen pointed out that 20 per cent of boys started smoking in the ninth grade, and almost 30 per cent of all girls smoke before they are graduated from high school.

We also know that this condition is being made continually worse under the promotional impact of advertising designed primarily to influence young people. Certainly the moral responsibility rests first on the tobacco manufacturer. Certainly it also rests on the advertising agencies. Certainly it also rests on the outstanding sports figures who permit their hero status to be prostituted. . . . But where others have persistently failed to subordinate their profit motives to the higher purpose of the general good health of our young people, then I think the broadcaster should make corrective moves on his own.

Collins, a reformed smoker himself and a maverick in the broadcasting industry, stirred such a storm with this speech that there were rumors that he would be asked to resign. But he stuck to his guns and, in December, called for an amendment to the NAB codes that would have set forth the general principle that "tobacco advertising having an especial appeal to minors, expressed or implied, should be avoided." At the same time, he labeled the Lucky Strike commercial designed to "Separate the Men from the Boys . . . but Not from the Girls" a "brazen, cynical flouting of concern of millions of American parents about their children starting the smoking habit." The responsible ad agency, Batten, Barton, Durstine, and Osborn, had no comment. In January, 1963, the NAB, having ironed out its internal differences over the Collins statements, extended his term as president for another three years. Having been considerably criticized, Collins said then the NAB would study the Surgeon General's report when it came out. About this time, Canadian cigarette-manufacturers decided to shift their commercials to the after-9-P.M. hours on radio and television to keep youngsters from seeing or hearing them.

The Surgeon General held his committee in high esteem and worked closely with it for fourteen months. Within sixteen days of the projected completion of its work, he personally accepted the draft report, although his department chiefs were less than enthusiastic about its political implications. After reviewing some 11,000 scientific reports and interviewing hundreds of witnesses, the panel's report was printed by the Government Printing Office at its old red-brick building in downtown Washington under security arrangements as tight as those covering proceedings of the National Security Council.

On a Saturday, January 11, 1964, when the stock market was closed, a news conference was called behind closed doors in the large State Department auditorium that President Kennedy used for his news conferences. There were "No Smoking" signs on both sides of the raised platform where the Surgeon General and his committee took seats. With television newsreel cameras in place, copies of the 387-page, brown-covered report, *Smoking and Health,* were handed out to the assembled members of the press. Reporters were given ninety minutes to read it and ask questions. Then, the doors of the auditorium were thrown open and the results of the study were telegraphed around the world. It was ten years from the time the smoking health issue had first burst upon the public view.

The committee concluded unanimously that: "Cigarette smoking is a health hazard of sufficient importance in the United States to warrant appropriate remedial action." It linked smoking causally with lung cancer and said it was a contributing factor in emphysema and chronic bronchitis as well as cancer of the mouth, throat, respiratory tract, and especially the larynx. Smoking also was linked with the increase in the death rates from lung cancer, emphysema, and chronic bronchitis. Detailed summaries of the studies reviewed by the committee indicated that although smoking was related to higher death rates from cardiovascular diseases and cirrhosis of the liver, a causal relationship had not been definitely established in those cases. Concluding the section on lung cancer, *Smoking and Health* said: "Cigarette smoking is causally related to lung cancer in men; the magnitude of the effect of cigarette smoking far outweighs all other factors. The data for women, though less extensive, point in the same direction."

The report went on to say that the risk of developing lung cancer increases with the duration of smoking and the number of cigarettes smoked each day and is diminished by discontinuing smoking. "The risk for developing cancer of the lung for the combined group of pipe smokers, cigar smokers, and pipe and cigar smokers is greater than in nonsmokers, but much less than for cigarette smokers," the report stated. "The data are insufficient to warrant a conclusion for each group individually."

As to why people smoke, the members of the Surgeon General's Advisory Committee concluded that the habitual use of tobacco is related primarily to psychological and social drives, reinforced and perpetuated by the pharmacological action of nicotine on the central nervous system.

Under questioning by newsmen, the Surgeon General said that the precise role of smoking in causing chronic diseases was not established by the studies. But the committee had come to the conclusion that it was better, from a public-health standpoint, to accept the causative effect the data indicated than to wait until the exact relationship had been established before taking any action.

Many Americans were startled, even frightened, at this condemnation of smoking. Cigarette sales dropped sharply. There was a run on antismoking drugs, clinics, and how-to-stop-smoking books. Some 25 per cent of American smokers either put out their cigarettes or cut down. The board of directors of the American Cancer Society hailed the Surgeon General's Advisory Committee Report as "a landmark in the history of man's fight against disease" and reaffirmed its position against prohibition of cigarettes, pointing out that while the individual must make his own decision about smoking, "he must have complete and true information about the health hazards of cigarette smoking."

Acting on the advice of his own committee, Dr. Terry moved to clean his own house. Distribution of cigarettes in the sixteen public hospitals and fifty Indian hospitals under the direction of the PHS was halted. Staff members at these hospitals were ordered to conduct educational programs to discourage smoking. The impact of the Surgeon General's Advisory Committee Report was such that other government agencies also rallied quickly behind the anti-smoking cause. Issuance of what began to be called the "Terry Report" gave the Federal Trade Commission a mandate to act.

Precisely one week after the Surgeon General made public his advisory committee's recommendations, the FTC announced that it would issue rules covering cigarette labeling and advertising. In its notice of rule-making, the commission said it was concerned with two ways in which cigarette advertising might be unlawfully misrepresenting or concealing the health hazards of smoking: first, that current ads give the false impression that smoking promotes health or physical well-being or is not a health hazard; second, that cigarette advertising creates a psychological and social barrier to the consuming public's understanding and appreciation of the gravity of the risks to life and health involved in cigarette-smoking. To correct this situation, the FTC proposed a health warning on cigarette packages and in advertising, saying: "Massive advertising, depicting and constantly reiterating the pleasures and desirability of cigarette smoking but failing to disclose the risks to health, appears to be a potent force in increasing sales of cigarettes, despite increasing scientific and governmental recognition of the existence and seriousness of such perils."

The FTC noted that, despite the accumulated evidence, since 1954 the annual consumption of cigarettes per person had steadily and sharply increased, from fewer than 3,400 in 1954 to more than 4,000 in 1963. In the same period, the total number of cigarettes sold to the public increased from about 380 billion to about 520 billion. Meanwhile, total advertising expenditures by the industry appeared to have doubled in this period, exceeding $200 million in 1963. The tobacco manufacturers and the public were given two months to comment on the proposed rules.

In a speech to the National Press Club, Surgeon General Terry said: "We intend to support the Federal Trade Commission in their proposed actions—because we are convinced that the American people have been deceived and misled by cigarette advertising—and their health has been harmed as a consequence."

Dr. Terry also reconvened the four voluntary agencies to discuss with them and other health agencies means of implementing the advisory committee report. At this meeting, a resolution was passed citing the need for coordinated national effort to achieve the "remedial action." A planning committee was established to suggest how this might best be done. The planning committee met in March and April and decided that a formal organization should be established with representation not only from health agencies but educational and youth-leadership organizations.

The Surgeon General's Advisory Committee Report seemed to be all that the antismoking forces could have hoped for. By bringing the issue into full public view, the advisory committee dealt the tobacco subsystem a forceful blow. But the threat of requiring a health warning had a strong, immediate effect on tobacco politics. Soon after the FTC announced its plans, both the House Committee on Interstate and Foreign Commerce and the Senate Committee on Commerce announced that they would hold hearings on the cigarette-health question. And when the bureaucracy began to act in league with Congress, the gentlemanly ways of tobacco politics changed almost overnight.

♣ 9

On Top of Old Smoking, Briefly

DESPITE THE SECRECY surrounding the Surgeon General's Advisory Committee Report, many people pretty much anticipated what it would say. Some acted on their foregone conclusions. Only a week before the government's report on smoking was issued, the American Tobacco Company, manufacturer of the top-selling Pall Mall, announced that it was putting a new low-tar filter cigarette on the market—the Carlton.

In an interview, Robert B. Walker, American Tobacco's president of less than one year, said: "We have to face the facts of life. Filter cigarettes are enjoying a growing share of the market. I intend to get our share." He added that "We should have gone into the filter market with both feet. Unfortunately, past management was not as farsighted in this respect as it might have been." The timing of American Tobacco's announcement was obviously intended to indicate that the company was not reacting to the "health scare" by marketing a filter cigarette—it was simply responding to the preference of smokers. But the Surgeon General's Advisory Committee Report must have had something to do with development of the new brand. The Carlton had not even been market tested before being

put on the market. "If you have a product with the attri-
butes that are desired," Mr. Walker, a chain smoker, told
the *New York Times,* "there is a good chance you can omit
test-marketing."

Almost all of the companies also boosted the amount of
their advertising. Possibly in consequence, fear generated
among smokers by the Surgeon General's Advisory Committee Report soon wore off. The Internal Revenue Service reported that cigarette sales shot up sharply in April,
following what had been a severe falling off. By the end of
what had looked like doomsday year, the industry believed
it was within 2 or 3 per cent of its previous record sales.

"April sales of P. Lorillard Co. are running ahead of
last year's, following a 'low point' in February—thanks
in part to 'record levels of advertising,' " Morton J. Cra-
mer, president, told his company's annual meeting. Because of the Surgeon General's Advisory Committee Report
and "competitive considerations," Lorillard's advertising
reached record levels during the first quarter, Mr. Cra-
mer said, adding that the decision to spend these record
amounts was made "in the full knowledge that commit-
ments of this magnitude would significantly affect our
already depressed earnings." The decision, he concluded,
"had already been proved sound—by the turnaround in
sales."

Behind the scenes, too, there had been a lot of activity,
even before the Surgeon General's Advisory Committee
Report came out. The industry was ready for action. Crucial decisions remained to be made, but the machinery had
been created to put up a fight on all fronts. Sometime late
in 1963, the prestigious Washington law firm of Arnold,
Fortas, & Porter had been called into the picture as counsel
to Philip Morris, and the firm's Abe Fortas, a senior partner, had been chosen by the six major tobacco companies to

form a committee of lawyers from his own and other top Washington law firms to solidify industry togetherness. They were to shape strategy and carry it out. Paul Porter spoke for his firm in the tobacco fight, while his partner Fortas, a friend and confidant of President Lyndon B. Johnson who later became the President's choice for the Supreme Court, stayed in the background.

One of the first decisions that faced the tobacco industry was whether to fight the FTC's proposed rules in the courts or seek relief from Congress. The lawyers' committee could provide the legal brainwork, but expert political advice was also needed. To help plan a careful and forceful campaign to save the industry from any governmental action that might be harmful to sales, the major six selected Earle C. Clements as their lobbyist. Clements had represented Kentucky in both the House and Senate and had the closest possible relationship with the LBJ White House. As an alumnus of Congress, Clements had floor privileges —an advantage that was to serve him well. The ties with President Johnson went back more than a decade. In 1951, Clements, then junior senator from Kentucky, was placed on the powerful Senate Democratic Policy Committee at the urging of Senator Johnson, and under Johnson's leadership, the Senate Democrats later accepted Clements, who has established himself as a liberal, first as minority whip and then as majority whip. When Johnson suffered a heart attack in 1955, Clements became acting majority leader, but lost his bid for re-election in 1956. During the 1960 Presidential election campaign, Clements attempted to gather political support for Johnson when it became apparent that Hubert Humphrey's bid for the Democratic Presidential nomination had failed. Clements also had another, unique tie to the White House. His daughter, Bess Abell, served as Lady Bird Johnson's social secretary.

Not only were Clements's political credentials impeccable, but he had the courtly manners of the Southern gentleman, suitable to the role of gentle persuader, as well as a horse-trader's sense for a deal. His old pals on Capitol Hill gave him credit for the shrewd decision that it would be better tactics for the tobacco industry to go to Congress and accept a package warning, if necessary, rather than to risk an FTC-imposed requirement that all advertisements carry a health warning too. State regulation (as in the antismoking heat of the early 1900's) was also a threat, and federal legislation would preempt the field. Moreover, the industry was not unaware that a package warning might serve as a legal defense. Hence the decision to remove the entire matter to Congress. It was apparently Clements who persuaded Oren D. Harris, the Arkansas Democrat who then served as chairman of the House Interstate and Foreign Commerce Committee, to hold hearings before the FTC Commerce Committee and to hold these hearings before the FTC had a chance to announce its decision on the proposed cigarette rules.

The industry thus went to FTC public hearings in March with a carefully laid plan aimed at transferring the problem to Congress, where it had reason to expect better treatment than the regulatory agency might give it. The agency had received more than 500 letters and other documents from physicians and other scientists, lawyers, psychologists, consumer groups, and individuals who wanted to be heard. Some came from high school students who had seen antismoking movies. Parents also wrote in to express hope that the government would do something to keep cigarettes from their children. The FTC's Bureau of Economics prepared and submitted a 288-page report on the tobacco industry, its role in the American economy, and cigarette advertising. Six volumes of cigarette advertisements were also placed in the record.

On March 16, 1964, the five FTC commissioners took their seats in the agency's wood-paneled hearing room in its headquarters building, which forms the apex of the Federal Triangle. The commissioners sat at a raised bench, in front of which there were counsel tables, a small table for the official recorder, and a podium on which witnesses could rest their notes. Rows of seats for spectators and participants in the hearing filled out the rest of the room. It was unusual for the commissioners to be present at rule-making sessions. But the FTC commissioners personally presided at the cigarette hearings. Four of the five favored the FTC-proposed rule. They were: Chairman Dixon; John Reilly, a Kennedy appointee who had worked with Attorney General Robert F. Kennedy at the Justice Department; Philip Elman, also a former Justice Department lawyer who had clerked for Supreme Court Justice Felix Frankfurter; and Mary Gardiner Jones, first woman ever appointed to the FTC. Miss Jones, a Republican who had been on the antitrust staff of the Justice Department's New York office, had been appointed to the FTC by President Johnson. Commissioner Everett A. MacIntyre, a native of North Carolina who had been on the staff of the FTC for many years before he was made a commissioner by President Kennedy, was not a strong supporter of the rule as written by the FTC staff. He favored negotiation with the tobacco industry.

Chairman Dixon, gray-haired, burly, and outspoken, called as the first of twenty-nine scheduled witnesses an assistant surgeon general, who was followed by Senator Neuberger. A spokesman for the Tobacco Institute came next, and after that, two university scientists who favored the proposed rule. Chairman Dixon invited each witness to read or submit a statement for the record. Some witnesses were then asked questions by the commissioners. Tension mounted in the hearing room when industry representatives rose to oppose the proposed FTC rules. Friendly witnesses were given prime time in terms of publicity. They were scheduled during the early hours when the press was looking for story leads. The hearings thus opened with two strong statements for the proposed rule. On the second day, marketing experts, scientists, and representatives of the tobacco-growers and advertising agencies appeared.

The tobacco industry might have chosen to ignore or downgrade the FTC action by electing not to send a personal representative to the hearings. But the Tobacco Institute chose, instead, to send a senior member of one of Washington's largest law firms. Attorney H. Thomas Austern, a partner in Dean Acheson's firm, Covington and Burling, argued that the commission did not have general rule-making powers of the kind it was attempting to exercise in the cigarette proceeding. Austern thus laid the legal groundwork for a court test of FTC authority should the tactic of halting the FTC in Congress prove unsuccessful. As the commissioners, who were themselves lawyers, listened to Austern's arguments, they became irritated. By the second day of the hearings, their patience was wearing thin. When Gilbert H. Weil, a representative of the Association of National Advertisers, took up the Tobacco Institute argument, Commissioner Elman made this response:

> Lawyers apparently feel that all law is divided into either substantive or procedural, or legislative, executive, and judicial, and, therefore, they have to talk in those terms.

And a lot of lawyers apparently have not read what the Supreme Court and what other students of the administrative process have written on the nature of administrative rule-making. I suggest you lawyers read these cases and come to us with a more realistic approach to the real problem, that we have here—instead of talking about fantasies and fictions. . . .

Suppose there is a product in general use throughout the United States . . . and suppose scientific research should conclusively establish that that product induced sterility. Would you say that under the Federal Trade Commission Act the only way in which this Commission could proceed to carry out its responsibilities of preventing deception . . . is to issue a complaint and a cease-and-desist order against each of the thousands and thousands of manufacturers? Or has Congress allowed us an alternative method of proceeding?

The American Medical Association opposed the FTC's proposed health warning. An AMA spokesman, F. J. L. Blasingame, said that "the health hazards of excessive smoking have been well publicized for more than ten years and are common knowledge. . . . We do not believe that the answer to the cigarette problem lies in cautionary labeling requirements. Experience in other countries indicates that the effect of such labeling at best is only to reduce temporarily the consumption of cigarettes. After a while the habitual smoker ignores the cautions expressed on the label." He also referred to the action of the AMA's House of Delegates when, in December, 1963, it approved an intensive research program

to probe beyond statistical evidence, to search for answers not now available to such questions as which disease in man may be caused or induced by the use of tobacco. Determination needs to be made whether some element or elements in smoke may be a direct or aggravating cause of cancer and other diseases and to identify these substances chemically. Questions of constitutional and physiologic factors, of physiological dependence, and of habituation require answers. Continuing and further clinical and pathologic studies need to be made along with collection and correlation of statistical data as it is collected to establish what relationships exist between the use of tobacco and disease. Since smoking may produce a tranquilizing effect as well as other favorable psychic reactions not so well identified, these factors need further study in evaluating the whole matter of the relationship of tobacco and disease.

The AMA's December action had been implemented in January. And in a show of sweet reasonableness, the tobacco industry's big six had declared that they would support AMA-sponsored research to the extent of $10 million over a five-year period.

On the third and last day of the FTC hearings, the governors of the tobacco states and their representatives and four members of the North Carolina congressional delegation appeared. These men had little choice but to support tobacco interests. They hoped the question would be removed to Congress.

Within a month after the conclusion of the hearings, the industry announced that it was going to have a go at self-regulation of cigarette advertising and soon thereafter adopted a voluntary code similar to the code of the National Association of Broadcasters. To demonstrate their seriousness, in June, 1964, the cigarette-makers hired former New Jersey Governor Robert B. Meyner to administer the Cigarette Advertising Code and gave him authority to fine violators up to $100,000. The companies, with Meyner as overseer, pledged to stop saying or implying that smoking is good for your health and to stop advertising in college newspapers or comic books or on "primarily" children's programs. Use of athletes was banned in advertising (and a hearty source of income thereby shut out for Phil Rizzuto, Richie Ashburn, Bobby Thompson, and others). The code also attempted to reduce representations that connect smoking with sexual or social conquests and acts requiring physical stamina. In the face of growing public pressures, in June, 1964, the cigarette manufacturers decided to drop virtually all cigarette advertising in college newspapers, magazines, and football programs. Campus promotional activity was also halted.

That summer, about two months after the public hearings, the FTC ruled that henceforth it would be an "unfair or deceptive practice" for any manufacturer "to fail to disclose, clearly and prominently, in all advertising and on every pack, box, carton or other container in which cigarettes are sold . . . that cigarette smoking is dangerous to health and may cause death from cancer and other diseases."

The commission said that when viewers witness "continued and unrestricted dissemination of cigarette advertising on radio and television and in other media, their natural, instinctive reaction is that the danger of cigarette smoking cannot be an established fact—else government would take steps to restrict cigarette advertising, and, specifically, would require that such advertising include a disclosure of the danger." The FTC also pointed out that while alcohol in moderation is not generally considered deleterious to health, advertisements for hard liquor are not broadcast on radio or television, that liquor advertising has consistently eschewed the themes of romance, contentment, and sociability that figure so prominently in cigarette advertising, and that alcoholic beverages are labeled to disclose the alcoholic content.

"A particularly important consideration" in its proceeding was the impact of cigarette advertising on young people, the FTC said. According to available data, it said, "smoking patterns indicate that an increasing proportion of persons in younger age groups are becoming regular smokers." And, because of the magnitude and pervasiveness of cigarette advertising, virtually all Americans, including most children, are continually exposed to the portrayal of the desirability of smoking and to assurances respecting the safety or healthfulness of cigarette smoking. Audience data for network television advertising, according to the commission, indicated that substantial numbers of children under eighteen years of age are exposed to such advertising. It was estimated that during a single evening time period, 46 per cent of the population thirteen to seventeen years of age, and 26 per cent of the population two to twelve years of age, were exposed to cigarette advertising.

The cigarette ruling was supposed to take effect on January 1, 1965. Commissioner MacIntyre, in a statement of disagreement with the FTC majority, said he would have delayed the effective date six months to give all parties more time to work out an effective solution.

In June, Surgeon General Terry proclaimed an "era of action" to change the smoking habits of the nation. Addressing a two-day National Conference on "Cigarette Smoking and Youth" convened by the voluntary health agencies in New York City, Dr. Terry warned that it might take ten years or more but that "no reasonable person" should dispute that cigarette-smoking is a serious health hazard. "None of us is about to be misled by the half-truth that we need more research before we can take action," he said. Dr. Terry outlined a wide range of plans and current activities aimed at understanding why youngsters take up smoking and how they can be dissuaded from doing so. "If this generation of children and youth takes up smoking, as they assuredly will unless they are convinced otherwise, millions of them in later years will suffer needless illness and disability, and will die before their time." Addressing an audience at the Hotel Biltmore, Dr. Terry said, "I ask you in all earnestness, can this generation of adults stand idly by and let this preventable mass tragedy unfold?"

A month later, as a result of meetings between Surgeon General Terry and the voluntary health agencies, the first broad-based campaign to discourage smoking was launched. The National Interagency Council on Smoking and Health was set up as an unusual coalition of government agencies and nongovernment organizations. Emerson Foote, former chairman of the McCann-Erickson ad agency in New York, became its first chairman. He took the job without pay and set up an office in New York. Foote believed in eliminating advertising as a necessary curb to smoking. "As long as you have cigarette companies . . . advertising showing healthy people enjoying their smokes, making speeches is not going to do any good," he said.

Congress reacted quickly to the FTC's newly promulgated rule. But even before the FTC announced its decision, there had been one bit of congressional activity that shook the confidence of tobacco industry leaders in the ability of Congress to kill any serious government attempts to interfere with their business. Shortly before the FTC held its public hearings, an amendment was attached to a crop-support bill in the Senate that would have abolished the tobacco-support and acreage-control programs. The amendment was defeated easily, by a vote of sixty-three to twenty-six, but it signaled the tobacco lobby that it would have to move forcefully.

After the FTC announcement was made, members introduced thirty-one bills in the House and four in the Senate. All of the Senate bills were intended to support the FTC and strengthen government regulatory powers over cigarette-makers. In the House, which usually responds more sensitively to special-interest pressures than the Senate, six bills would have stripped the FTC of its powers to regulate cigarette advertising. The remaining twenty-five bills would have set up government research programs or strengthened the FTC. But this was not a true indication of congressional reaction. It quickly became apparent from speeches on the floor that the FTC's bold step would meet tough opposition.

The Harris hearings opened in late June with a bit of theatrics. Representative Horace R. Kornegay, a Democratic committeeman from tobacco-dependent North Carolina, brought a potted tobacco plant into the opening session of the House Commerce Committee hearings. "This tobacco plant stands as the defendant in this trial," Kornegay declared. "This plant and millions of Americans stand in serious jeopardy today. The health factor is tremendously important . . . there is a definite need for more research to find out what, if any, health hazards exist. . . . Let's give it a fair trial." Congressman Kornegay, who later became president of the Tobacco Institute, was to prove a staunch friend of the tobacco interests.

An internal government dispute over cigarette-smoking also erupted on the first day of the hearings. It was revealed that Surgeon General Terry had made a late bid for Food and Drug Administration authority to regulate health-hazard labelings on cigarettes. His proposal had followed a protest against any such action by Senator Maurine Neuberger, who said she had only recently become aware that such a move was contemplated. She said the decision of the Health, Education, and Welfare Department to request jurisdiction marked an "ironic twist." Mrs. Neuberger testified that on January 28, 1963, she wrote to FDA Commissioner George P. Larrick suggesting that the FDA had authority to control cigarette labels under the federal

Hazardous Substances Labeling Act of 1960 and that Commissioner Larrick disagreed. "One wonders just how serious the Department's urge to regulate really is," she said. "I fail to see why, at this late date, HEW now feels its jurisdictional toes have been trodden on. In any event, it would be tragic if regulations so significant to the health of Americans should fall prey to a petty jurisdictional dispute." The Surgeon General's proposal would have let Congress set the policy on whether cigarette packages should carry health-hazard warnings. If Congress so decreed, he said, machinery was available in the FDA to enforce labeling regulations.

When House Commerce Committee members raised the possibility that the advertising ruling might never be put into effect, FTC Chairman Dixon replied that the rule might not be necessary if the industry adopted an effective voluntary program. Among those who testified that they would support court challenges of the FTC ruling were Governor Terry Sanford and Democratic Senators B. Everett Jordan and Sam J. Ervin—all of North Carolina. Representative L. H. Fountain, another North Carolina Democrat, called the FTC regulation "capricious, arbitrary, unreasonable, and unsupported by fact." It was generally conceded that any legislation to regulate cigarette advertising would face an uphill fight in both houses of Congress.

The tobacco industry scored one immediate success, in which the influence of Earle Clements could be clearly seen. The committee asked the FTC to delay the effect of its rulings, since Congress would not have time to act by the end of the session. The labeling rule was to have gone into effect on January 1, 1965, and the advertising rule six months later. The FTC complied with the request, pushing the effective date for both regulations back to July 1. So the stage was set for the 1965 fight in Congress.

In December, the President's Commission on Heart Disease, Cancer, and Stroke called for a large-scale government educational spending campaign in the health field—with special emphasis on the hazards of smoking. The twenty-five-member panel said that the three killer diseases accounted for 70 per cent of deaths in America every year. Its plan called for underwriting the production of twelve half-hour documentary films and the expenditure of $10 million over a three-year period on antismoking education. The commission said that such a program would cut down on cancer and cardiovascular disease. This call was ignored by Congress, which had already rejected a $1.9 million appropriation for the Public Health Service to begin an antismoking campaign and set up a network of smoking control clinics. Congress voted on that appropriation after forty-two House members from tobacco states signed a petition against it.

Also in December, 1964, the *New York Times* carried an editorial saying that every package of cigarettes should carry a health warning. The *Times,* which had carried $400,000 worth of cigarette advertising in the eleven preceding months of the year, went on to say: "The trouble is that the facts have been blurred and buried by the constant avalanche of cigarette advertisements."

That same month, at the Public Health Service's annual Christmas party, some of the agency's employees entertained their colleagues by singing their own version of "On Top of Old Smoky." Their boss, the Surgeon General, had warned that "cigarette smoking was a health hazard of sufficient importance to warrant 'remedial action.' " Twelve months had passed, and no such action had been taken.

"On top of Old Smoking," they sang, "A year has gone by/But the smoke we're deploring/Still gets in your eye."

♣ 10

1965: Congress and the Cigarette

WHEN THE NEW CONGRESS OPENED in 1965, the tobacco manufacturers were playing it cool. Their lobbyist, Earle C. Clements, the former Democratic Senator from Kentucky, had advised them to play down the health issue, emphasize the importance of cigarettes in the nation's economy, remind the media of their financial stake in cigarette advertising, oppose all regulatory legislation but settle for a package warning if they had to give in on something. Above all, the Federal Trade Commission must be blocked from requiring an advertising warning. The cigarette-makers sensed that tobacco's political-bureaucratic subsystem had begun to break down. They moved with sensitivity to make the best of a weakened position. Primarily, they wanted to head off any action that could hurt cigarette sales. Having adopted the Clements strategy, they were calmly awaiting developments.

As the fateful year of 1965 approached, the tobacco industry was in a position of strength, with the bureaucracy bickering and the White House silent. Although President Johnson had a mechanism in his Executive Office's Bureau of the Budget to coordinate policy on the cigarette-health matter, he chose not to use it. Instead of performing a coordinating function, the Bureau allowed all agency letters —either favoring or opposing a health warning—to go straight up to Congress. When Johnson delivered his State of the Union Message at the opening of Congress in January, it contained a number of health proposals but no mention of the smoking question.

That part of the bureaucracy which favored regulation could not be expected to carry the battle too far alone. The Public Health Service, lacking true friends in Congress, attempted to pull together support outside government. The National Interagency Council on Smoking and Health drummed up some support from state health societies, which produced additional mail to congressmen urging them to hold to the FTC advertising rule. The FTC itself was in a poor position to take on Congress. Having already started an action that was looked on with disfavor by powerful elements in Congress, it could hardly be expected to stick its neck out even further. The independent regulatory commissions, and their executives, like Chairman Dixon, are considered arms of Congress. They must follow the lead of Congress if controversy arises.

The Department of Agriculture also found itself in a tight spot. Pressed by reporters who questioned him about the continuation of tobacco price supports in the face of health revelations, Agriculture Secretary Orville Freeman on a notable occasion already had come up with a political classic. He propounded the theory that if price supports were discontinued, cigarettes would cost less and people would smoke more. Hence, supports should be maintained. Later, the Department of Agriculture took an official position against the inclusion of a health warning on packages or in advertising. Commenting on the pending legislation in a letter to Senator Warren G. Magnuson (D., Washington), a department spokesman said: "Much more explicit identification of the constituents of tobacco smoke and more complete understanding of their role as related to health must be sought and achieved. Only this will provide an adequate basis for deciding whether or not such stringent provisions as those in [the bill, which required only the health warning on packages] are warranted." Thus was the bureaucracy split at a crucial time.

The antismoking forces had gathered strength from the Surgeon General's Advisory Committee Report. The health groups that rallied around the Surgeon General after release of the report found some public support on the state and local level. The health commissioner of New York City proposed cigarette-package warnings. New York State and Massachusetts were considering similar proposals. The governor of California had set up a cigarette-smoking advisory committee preparatory to taking regulatory action. Pressure was also growing in some areas to enforce laws already on the books barring cigarette sales to minors. The tobacco industry feared state regulation in terms of inconvenience as much as anything, since there could theoretically be as many labeling laws as there are states. But while tobacco-state congressmen had powerful reasons to reverse the FTC action, namely constituent support, there were no "health" congressmen. Members of Congress vote funds for health research with enthusiasm but then almost always find it difficult to act to reduce the hazards created by or identified with the health research they sponsor.

Earle Clements had been at work for almost a year to forge a united front in Congress. He had a lot going for him on Capitol Hill besides his own popularity. Tobacco had formidable power. Because of the system that awards committee chairmanships to senior members of Congress, and because of the essentially one-party system in the

South, members from the tobacco states held influential committee positions. In the Senate, nearly one-fourth of the committees were chaired by men from the six tobacco states. Of the twenty-one committees in the House, tobacco-state congressmen chaired seven. Both houses of Congress tend to follow the dictates of their committees—in whose meeting rooms the initial phase of the tobacco battle would be fought. There were other things working to preserve the *status quo*. On an issue of great importance to certain congressmen, the Southern bloc tends to pull together. Additionally, philosophical opposition to government regulation of business was expected to pull in a good number of Republican votes.

The tobacco interests were fairly confident that they would win the day in the House of Representatives, where the battle was due to begin. They had a good friend in Representative Oren D. Harris, chairman of the House Interstate and Foreign Commerce Committee. The committee itself was a fairly conservative force. Harris represented a rural area of Arkansas and the second-ranking member, Harley O. Staggers, came from a similar part of West Virginia. Seven other members of the thirty-three-member committee represented tobacco regions.

But while the House was considered friendly to tobacco interests, the real test of Clements's strategy lay in the Senate, where the tobacco people had to contend with a little band of liberals—among them, Senator Magnuson, who chaired the Commerce Committee. The Senate committee, generally more consumer-oriented than its House counterpart, had begun to develop and vote out a series of consumer-protection bills, but it was closely divided on the tobacco issue. Senator Maurine Neuberger, tobacco's biggest enemy in Congress, had won a seat on it when Congress opened in 1965. Chairman Magnuson was thus a crucial figure to both smoking and health forces. He was careful to avoid committing himself at an early date. But his inclinations were soon evident in the bill he sponsored. Of the many bills drafted, two came in for serious consideration by the Senate committee. They were S. 559, sponsored by Senator Magnuson, and S. 547, sponsored by Senator Neuberger. The Magnuson bill called for a package warning only, while Senator Neuberger's provided in addition for a warning in advertising.

When hearings got under way, all the familiar spokesmen for the voluntary health agencies appeared to testify on the evidence linking cigarette-smoking with a variety of diseases. It was brought out that the American Medical Association, through its House of Delegates, had approved a statement the previous June declaring that "cigarette smoking is a serious health hazard." Testifying on March 23, Dr. Thomas Carlile of Seattle, representing the American Cancer Society, noted that in England and Italy governmental controls had been imposed on cigarette advertising and that extensive programs of education on the danger of cigarette-smoking were being carried out in many countries, including England, Sweden, Russia, and the Netherlands. Winding up his testimony, Dr. Carlile, a radiologist at Seattle's Mason Clinic, said that for many years he had been a heavy smoker but that he had stopped "when one week in 1959 I had to examine the chest X-rays of two of my partners, both of whom were heavy smokers, both of whom had lung cancer, both of whom died of their disease within a period of six months."

There were light moments during the course of the hearings as the nicotian apocrypha was explored and revived. Dr. Oscar Auerbach, senior medical investigator for the Veterans Administration Hospital in East Orange, N.J., and professor of pathology at New York Medical College in New York City, described his research on lung cancer. Toward the end of his testimony, a typical colloquy took place. Senator Norris Cotton, New Hampshire Republican, said:

> As a young man I smoked cigars constantly, and I was constantly told by my grandfather, who was a clergyman, I was constantly reminded that General Grant died of throat cancer because he was such a constant cigar smoker. I don't suppose you ever treated General Grant?
>
> DR. AUERBACH: No, sir.
>
> (Laughter.)
>
> SENATOR COTTON: Is that just a legend?
>
> DR. AUERBACH: No, sir, it is not a legend. There are cases of lung cancer in individuals who smoked cigars only. There are cases of carcinoma of the larynx, carcinoma of the tongue, and carcinoma of the membranes of the mouth related to cigars. But by far the over-all important agent is the cigarette.

The National Interagency Council on Smoking and Health had a strong spokesman in Emerson Foote, the "reformed" smoker who had resigned as board chairman of McCann-Erickson, the New York ad agency, where he had handled the Lucky Strike account. Foote decided to join the health forces not, he explained, because he disliked smoking—"I am not against tobacco. I am against cancer, heart disease, and emphysema." Though he had written many—if not most—of the slogans that had made his client prosperous and helped popularize smoking, Foote took the position that no progress would be made on the antismoking front until cigarette advertising was made self-defeating. He therefore favored a health warning in advertising.

On the whole, the health groups behaved as if they thought there was little hope in the House of legislation supporting the FTC. They saved their energy for the Senate. And when he was sent up to Capitol Hill to testify during the House hearings, Surgeon General Terry, who had personally supported the report of his advisory committee, was obliged to state the position of his boss, the Secretary of Health, Education, and Welfare, which made it look as if the Public Health Service did not strongly favor legislation upholding the FTC.

Earle Clements, supported by congressmen from the tobacco states, touted the industry's case in congressional offices and cloakrooms. Also in the background helping Clements write testimony and prepare the industry's appeal to the courts, if that should become necessary, was that high-powered group of industry attorneys and Washington lawyers (including President Johnson's good friend Abe Fortas), that had been hired to represent the six leading cigarette-manufacturers. With the help of friendly congressmen, the industry carefully built a record designed to show that medical opinion was split over the "Terry Report"—despite the fact that no medical group had denied its validity.

The cigarette lobby's presentation before Congress differed radically from its strategy at the FTC hearings. Before the congressional committees, industry spokesmen covered all aspects of the argument: the Surgeon General's Advisory Committee Report, other studies on the health consequences of smoking, the importance of unfettered competition to the nation, and the proper role of Congress vis-à-vis the states and administrative agencies. This approach contrasted sharply with the limited legal argument presented at the FTC. In Congress, dozens of witnesses from a variety of professional skills appeared, their testimony skillfully orchestrated by Clements.

The heart of the industry case was given by Bowman Gray, board chairman of Reynolds. Acknowledging the health question, he spoke more in sorrow than anger. Gray proved a highly competent and effective witness. His voice never rose above a conversational tone. For two hours at the witness table, in both the House and Senate committees, he chain-smoked his way through the industry arguments. Although Gray disclaimed any medical expertise, he carefully laid the groundwork for the prosmoking medical arguments. He touched base with the economists by noting that "unwise legislation in this field could produce repercussions which would be felt throughout the country's economy." He went on to warn that the balance-of-payments problem might even be exacerbated if exports of tobacco products fell. Ideological and philosophical objections also appeared in his testimony. Policy in a democracy should be made by Congress, not an administrative agency, he argued. The right to advertise, he deemed "an essential commercial" right. Gray acknowledged that he believed the FTC rule was "step one in the [government's] trying to get control of one industry," and added, sounding a portentous note, that it would be a "first step to get control of other industries."

Bowman Gray thought the health warning unnecessary. But, if there had to be one, it should be phrased in a "fair and factual manner" and confined strictly to the package. Asked if the industry would continue advertising if a "self-defeating" warning notice had to be included in advertising, he replied: "I can't speak for the industry. I think we as a company would have to seriously consider discontinuing advertising under such circumstances." That remark was obviously aimed at the publishing and broadcast industries, which proved to be strong allies of tobacco—at that stage of the game, at least.

(The American Newspaper Publishers Association, the Advertising Federation of America, the Association of

National Advertising, the Radio Advertising Bureau, and the National Association of Broadcasters, in fact, did their own lobbying as legislation to overturn the FTC moved through Congress. It has been estimated that about one-third of the members of Congress own stock in radio and television stations. In any event, all congressmen are sensitive to the attitude of station-owners and newspapers.)

A parade of witnesses for the tobacco industry, the largest number of whom were medical doctors and professionals from allied fields, followed the masterful Bowman Gray. All of them cast doubt on the Surgeon General's Advisory Committee Report, claiming that it was based on statistical rather than clinical evidence and was not sufficient proof that smoking caused diseases. Darrell Huff, author of *How to Lie With Statistics* (New York: W. W. Norton, 1954), talked darkly about the advisory committee's work. He pointed to a number of statistical and methodological "warning signals" that in his view rendered some conclusions open to question. A Virginia pathologist argued that the evidence submitted by "proponents on the theory that lung cancer is caused by smoking . . . does not constitute scientific proof of this theory." The majority of witnesses at the congressional hearings testified against the Surgeon General's Advisory Committee Report and the Federal Trade Commission's proposed rules. Most of the professionals who testified identified their employers as independent research outfits.

Nearly two years after the hearings, it was disclosed that a few of the witnesses had not properly or fully identified themselves. Senator Daniel B. Brewster (D., Maryland) mailed questionnaires to those who testified on behalf of the cigarette industry. Sixteen of the thirty-seven questionnaires he sent were returned. Some of those answering admitted that they had received large fees from the tobacco interests for their testimony. Brewster's revelations came as a belated surprise to some members of the committee, who thought that they had heard professional opinions untarnished by any possible financial connection with the industry. Senator Brewster suggested that there be a committee investigation of any possible conflict of interest that might have arisen at the labeling hearings, but the request died quietly and quickly. Congress itself pays only the expenses of those witnesses it asks to testify; others pay their own expenses. The problem of witnesses paid by special interests is not serious so long as they disclose their connections. The problem of undisclosed connections is an ethical one; its implications remain unexplored by Congress. At the time Brewster made his disclosure, a lawyer representing the Tobacco Institute and three major cigarette-manufacturers protested that the payments represented "usual professional charges" and were, therefore, "entirely proper."

By the time Congress held its second round of hearings in 1965, the cigarette-manufacturers had been under self-regulation for a year. Former New Jersey Governor Meyner, administrator of the industry advertising code, had, by then, made many decisions, passing on everything from television commercials through the words on the pack itself to the actual name of the brand. It had been decided that manufacturers could not be expected to give up years of investment in a brand name. Thus, despite the health implications, U.S. Tobacco was allowed to keep the name Sano and Brown & Williamson the name Life. But Meyner had said "no" to claims in the area of mental health. Over the years, many advertisers had implied a powerful tranquilizing or antidepressant quality in their products. A group of commercials done in precode days for Spring cigarettes became known in the industry as the "suicide series"; typically, in their TV come-ons, the woman in an empty railroad station in the middle of the night appeared so intensely depressed that it seemed possible she would leap in front of a train before she had a chance to light up a Spring and snap out of her dark mood. Camel commercials showed the first draw virtually quieting hurricanes at sea. But Meyner found himself in something of a bind over the appeals of snobbishness, romance, masculinity, and youthful high spirits that, of course, attracted adults as well as adolescents. As long as this appeal was not directed blatantly at youth, he felt there was little he could do to control it. With the glamour of cigarettes smoking up TV screens every few minutes, the code had become something of a joke, but industry representatives were still referring to it as an effective step toward meeting criticism.

The House committee, quite predictably, voted out a bill to require a label on the side of the package but to bar the FTC permanently from requiring a warning in ads. During floor debate, Representative Walter E. Rogers (D., Texas) charged the FTC with trying to "run this country" and accused Dr. Terry of trying to "brainwash" the public and "destroy" the tobacco industry. Two other cheerleaders for the cigarette industry, Democrats Horace R. Kornegay and Harold D. Cooley, both from the tobacco-growing state of North Carolina, made emotional speeches about America's oldest industry, dating back to the days of Sir Walter Raleigh. On the other side of the issue, John Dingell (D., Michigan) told the House that Congressional inaction would force a later reappraisal of the "whole problem of tobacco" and Representative Philip Burton (D., California) demanded a roll-call vote. But Rogers and Harris passed the word to defeat it. Instead, there was only one teller vote. (Until change came with the Ninety-second Congress in 1971 a teller vote required that congressmen file down the aisle in full view of the galleries, but it did not require them to record their names and position. Now, they must show red or green cards that identify "yes" or "no" votes.)

The vote occurred on an amendment offered by James Roosevelt (D., California) to protect future state controls on the labeling and advertising of cigarettes. The bill favored by the tobacco lobby prohibited the FTC and state and local governments from taking regulatory action. During the course of debate, Representative Roosevelt declared: "We do not pre-empt the right of states to act on drug traffic. Why do we prohibit the states in the matter of cigarettes?" Representative Harris replied: "There are hundreds of drug manufacturers producing thousands of drugs. There are only a few cigarette manufacturers producing a comparatively small number of brands of cigarettes, sold throughout the fifty states." Here, Representative James C. Corman, another California Democrat, broke in: "Why are we pre-empting the authority of a regulatory body, the FTC, to make further studies and decisions, if more conclusive evidence on cigarette dangers is found?"

Not all the congressmen who supported the tobacco industry came out in the open. Some were afraid some future political opponent would accuse them of having voted for lung cancer. The teller vote, which preserved their anonymity, was taken while Representative John E. Moss (D., California), the only member of the Commerce Committee to dissent in its report, was absent from the chamber and therefore not able to lead the debate of the antismoking forces. The bill was brought to the floor on a Tuesday afternoon when only a few members were present. Moss, who had been on a trip to Europe, had been told that the vote would not come up until after his return on Thursday. It was in fact taken just half an hour before he landed at Dulles airport. Congressman Richard Bolling (D., Missouri) spoke of the questionable tactics of bringing the labeling bill to the floor early, saying: "The Committee [Interstate and Foreign Commerce] was able to get through this House of Representatives a piece of legislation which it agreed upon, when the only person who opposed the legislation strongly enough to sign a minority report was known to be away and unable to return."

Recognizing that the House was considerably more procigarette than the Senate, the antismoking lobbyists shifted the scene of their intense activity to the Senate. Mrs. Neuberger now had a chance to challenge the witnesses who appeared before the committee and to proselytize her colleagues. To offset attempts to undercut FTC rulings, she introduced legislation giving congressional sanction to what the FTC was trying to do. In this effort, she stood virtually alone.

Senator Neuberger faced a united Republican opposition under the leadership of Thruston Morton, the popular Senator from Kentucky. And two Democratic senators, Vance Hartke of Indiana and Ross Bass of Tennessee, were unsympathetic to the pleas of their female colleague. Senator Bass had a sizable tobacco constituency, and Senator Hartke was indebted to Earle Clements for his aid as director of the Senate Democratic Campaign Fund —the job Clements had taken on after his own defeat in 1956. Hartke, who was subject to no strong pressures from his constituency, said that he had come to the hearings thinking that there "must be some connection" between smoking and health but came away "completely astonished" to find that a connection had not been proven.

The six Republicans and two Democrats united in opposition to the Senator from Oregon and were supported by some wavering Democrats unenthusiastic about the health position.

The Senate Committee on Commerce voted down Mrs. Neuberger and the FTC's approach twelve to two and then proceeded to settle down to the real issue—how long to suspend the effect of the FTC's ruling on advertising. Chairman Magnuson and a number of the committee members were opposed to suspending the ruling permanently, as the House had done. Morton, Bass, and Hartke finally agreed with Magnuson to vote out a bill to require a label on packages by the following January and to suspend the advertising rule for three years after that. In the committee's report to the Senate, only Mrs. Neuberger objected. Because the bill was couched in the language of a public-health measure, a number of senators honestly believed that all they were about to take was the heroic step of warning the public about the health dangers in smoking. Last-minute efforts to explain what was actually involved—by Mrs. Neuberger, Senator Robert F. Kennedy, their aides, and David Cohen, lobbyist for the Americans for Democratic Action—failed. On July 6, 1965, the Senate went on to pass the bill by a vote of seventy-two to five, with most of the tobacco-state senators voting for it.

Four who aligned themselves against the bill were Democrats Paul Douglas of Illinois, Robert Kennedy of New York, Gaylord Nelson of Wisconsin, and Joseph Clark of Pennsylvania. The fifth opposing vote was cast by Republican Senator Wallace Bennett of Utah, a Mormon and a long-time foe of smoking. Even those states-rightists who often raise objections to bills that grant the national government additional powers were quiet on the labeling bill. There was no recorded Southern or conservative objection to the prohibition of state regulatory legislation.

Throughout the congressional proceedings, President Johnson maintained a conspicuous silence on the smoking issue. In all probability, the President did not want to take on a fight with members of his own party. There was speculation about the role of Abe Fortas. When the time came for key votes to be taken, Fortas was on the telephone. And when the Senate bill went into conference with the House, Fortas made calls on behalf of the House bill. Reportedly, there was one call from Fortas recorded at Magnuson's office on June 24, 1965: "He [Fortas] hopes you will go along with provisions of the House-passed bill."

But Magnuson did not follow Fortas's advice. The final legislation tied the hands of the FTC for only three years. Another important provision of the bill prohibited other federal agencies—for example, the Federal Communications Commission—from taking any action to require health warnings in advertising. State and local action was also blocked or pre-empted by congressional action. The House conferees would not accept the Senate provision that the health warning be placed on the front of the cigarette package. After some haggling, the conferees agreed to a requirement that the warning appear in a conspicuous place in "conspicuous and legible type." The Senate bill proposed a $100,000 fine for violation of the measure. The House bill carried a $10,000 penalty. The House provision was included in the compromise. The law was to be enforced by the Justice Department.

Eight disenchanted members of Congress tried to persuade President Johnson to veto the bill. Their efforts were to no avail. The President signed the legislation in the privacy of his office on July 27—with none of the publicity, none of the usual glitter and handing out of pens accompanying such occasions. Beginning January 1, 1966, the law said, all cigarette packages were required to carry the label: "Caution—cigarette smoking may be hazardous to your health."

The text of the Cigarette Labeling and Advertising Act of 1965 begins by declaring that it was the intention of Congress to establish a federal program to inform the public of the possible health hazards of smoking. To this end, Congress appropriated $2 million—less than one–one hundredth of what the cigarette companies were spending on TV and radio advertising—shortly after the labeling act was passed to establish the National Clearing-house for Smoking and Health. This agency was created as part of the Public Health Service to carry out educational campaigns and collect data on smoking-and-health research.

At first, opinions differed as to who "won" the 1965 battle. FTC chairman Dixon was inclined to the view that the package health warning was a step forward for which his agency could proudly take credit. But gradually it became clear that the tobacco industry could claim a solid victory. "The Congressional steamroller was never in higher gear than when the tobacco lobby rammed the so-called cigarette labeling bill through the House," columnist Drew Pearson wrote. The *New York Times* called the new law "a shocking piece of special-interest legislation . . . a bill to protect the economic health of the tobacco industry by freeing it of proper regulation," and editorialized that "The President and Congress [are] flashing a green signal to the lobbyists that any regulatory agency is open to invasion and emasculation."

The cigarette-manufacturers were jubilant. They did as

well as could have been expected under the circumstances. Maybe better. They got a bill they could live with. A health warning on cigarette packages might have been considered a defeat a couple of years earlier, but in 1965 it was seen as a triumph by the tobacco industry. After Congress slapped down the FTC, a grateful tobacco industry demonstrated its thanks and got up a kitty to be contributed to the re-election campaigns of deserving legislators. Most of it went to members of the House Commerce Committee.

Passage of the Cigarette Labeling and Advertising Act marked the end of a well-organized campaign to move Congress to adopt an unusual oversight measure. In the end, it was unmistakably clear where the real policy-making power lay. But the lengths to which Congress went to discipline the FTC were truly unusual. Even some supporters of the legislation now regard it as "the rape of 1965." Senator Frank E. Moss (D., Utah) observed in 1969 that "in retrospect, it was a tragic step backwards. . . . In exchange for eleven words on the side of the cigarette package, Congress exempted the cigarette industry from the normal regulatory processes of federal, state, and local regulations."

⚘ 11

Enter Banzhaf and His Bandits

As ALMOST EVERYONE PREDICTED, the package warning had little effect on the smoking habits of Americans. Sales held up well, and the industry continued to pour hundreds of millions of dollars into advertising. With expenditures by then of more than $200 million a year on radio and television alone, cigarette advertisers had become the single largest product advertisers on television, accounting for about 8 per cent of TV advertising time. If a health warning had been required in advertising, as the FTC proposed, cigarette advertising would almost certainly have left the airways in 1965. That threat to the cigarette people had been overcome for the time being. But from another, unexpected corner, a new threat appeared.

The era of the consumer had dawned and with it a new breed of crusader, the sophisticated young lawyer armed with little more than the tools of his trade. *Caveat emptor* was a thing of the past. "Industry beware" better suited the mood of the 1960's. John F. Banzhaf III, who has been called the "Ralph Nader of the tobacco industry," was a young man with an idea whose time had come.

Banzhaf had begun life as something of a prodigy, graduating from Stuyvesant High School in New York at the age of fifteen after skipping several grades. The tall, soft-spoken youth then entered Massachusetts Institute of Technology in electrical engineering. But he grew dissatisfied with the constraints of a scientific career and, having discovered that he enjoyed working with people, entered Columbia Law School after graduating from MIT. There he became a legal activist and a maverick member of the *Law Review* staff. And from there he took his first crack at the bureaucracy in Washington. During the course of some research, it occurred to young Banzhaf that no one ever had been given a copyright for a computer program. "So I sat down and wrote a couple and sent them to the copyright office," he recalls. "After some haggling on both sides, the copyright office for the very first time wrote a copyright for computer programs."

This event in the life of John Banzhaf gave him his first publicity—a story in the *New York Times* accompanied by his picture. He liked the experience and was spurred to further action. Since Congress was considering a copyright revision law, he asked for permission to testify. To his surprise, his request was granted and congressmen listened attentively. Eventually, Congress decided to study the use of copyright materials in computer-data storage and retrieval systems. Banzhaf turned next to the question of reapportionment and the electoral college system and entered several reapportionment cases as a friend of the court. The reawakening of interest in direct election of the President is partly the result of his efforts, Banzhaf feels. After graduating from Columbia *magna cum laude,* Banzhaf spent the summer working on the social staff of a cruise ship during his summer vacation, before putting in a tough year as law clerk for Judge Spottswood W. Robinson of the U.S. District Court for the District of Columbia. Then, on a Thanksgiving day in 1966 that the

American tobacco industry has reason to regret, while he was watching a football game at his parents' home in the Bronx, the network interrupted several times with a commercial showing rugged men smoking cigarettes in a hearty Western setting. The commercial implied that any man who wanted to be truly masculine had to smoke cigarettes. It occurred to Banzhaf that what he was seeing might be considered legally "controversial."

Theoretically, at least, anyone can buy a printing press and publish a newspaper or magazine. Not just anyone can find himself a frequency and broadcast. There are only a certain number of radio frequencies and television channels, and they must be allocated in some way. This task has logically fallen to the federal government, which regulates broadcasting as a public-service industry. The recipients of broadcast licenses must, therefore, operate in the public interest. They must, among other things, present "a fair cross section of opinion in the coverage of public affairs and matters of public controversy." That is what John Banzhaf had in mind as he sat before the family television set. If cigarette-smoking was controversial, couldn't broadcasters be required to give the other side of the story if they took cigarette commercials?

Banzhaf, who, unlike fellow consumer advocate Ralph Nader, likes the good life and does not deny himself the creature comforts, was preparing to go off on another cruise. But he followed up on his inspiration immediately. He wrote to television station WCBS-TV in New York requesting that he or some other responsible spokesman be given an opportunity "to present contrasting views on the issue of the benefits and advisability of smoking." His letter cited three commercials over WCBS-TV that presented the view that smoking is "socially acceptable and desirable, manly, and a necessary part of a rich full life." In his letter of December 1, 1966, he asked free time roughly approximate to that spent on the promotion of "the virtues and values of smoking." CBS routinely turned down the request. In late December, he shot off a second letter to CBS, and, on January 5, in the purser's office of the Swedish-American Line's M.S. *Kungsholm,* Banzhaf typed up a formal complaint against WCBS-TV and mailed it to the Federal Communications Commission in Washington.

The tanned and rested Banzhaf returned to New York from a ninety-two-day cruise of the South Seas to join a New York patent law firm. He appeared to be on the way to a successful career as a New York lawyer when, to his amazement, just two weeks after his new job had started, the FCC upheld his complaint. In a letter to television station WCBS-TV dated June 2, 1967, the commission said programs it had broadcast dealing with the effect of smoking on health were insufficient to offset the effects of paid advertisements broadcast for a total of five to ten minutes each broadcast day. "We hold that the fairness doctrine is applicable to such advertisements," the commission said in a letter signed by Ben F. Waple, FCC Secretary.

The FCC rejected Banzhaf's claim for equal time, however. "The practical result of any roughly one-to-one correlation would probably be either the elimination or substantial curtailment of broadcast cigarette advertising," the regulatory agency said. The FCC called on the station to provide free each week "a significant amount of time for the other viewpoint," thereby implementing the smoking education campaigns launched by the government under the cigarette labeling law. "This requirement will not preclude or curtail presentation by stations of cigarette advertising which they choose to carry."

The decision of the FCC, which had often been accused of being too solicitous of the industry it regulates, came as a surprise to everyone, including tobacco-state congressmen. The tobacco industry and the broadcasters expressed shock. The president of the National Association of Broadcasters called the action an "unwarranted and dangerous intrusion into American business." Congressman Walter Jones, a North Carolina Democrat, tried to rally support for the cigarette-makers, among other businessmen, by claiming that they, too, could meet the same fate at the hands of the FCC. He warned that other groups, including those opposing consumption of alcoholic beverages, might have the fairness doctrine applied to them. "What if a group claims automobiles are unsafe and candy and soda rot your teeth?" asked one network official. "Where does it stop?"

The FCC was deluged with requests to reconsider its action. But on the second go-round, the agency stood firm in its unanimous decision. The seven members of the FCC, including Chairman Rosel Hyde, who had generally been considered pro-industry, apparently felt that they were in the presence of something evil that had to be eliminated from American life. Hyde's attitude *may* have been influenced by his religion, some of his associates surmised. He is a member of the Mormon church, which prohibits smoking. But much of the impetus within the FCC came from its general counsel, Henry Geller, who warned: "A station's record in the area will be taken into consideration at license-renewal time."

Television viewers were already familiar with the grim antismoking messages sponsored by the American Cancer Society. As a result of the FCC ruling, many of the voluntary health agencies and the Public Health Service made available to the television and radio industries spot announcements and other program materials on the serious consequences to health caused by cigarette-smoking. The public-health campaign to dissuade 50 million American cigarette-smokers from the habit was transformed overnight into a hard sell.

Some of the health groups, elated at first, began to have qualms when the tobacco and broadcast industries tried to have the FCC ruling overturned in the courts. The misgivings of groups like the American Cancer Society were based on the fear that the courts might agree to dismiss the FCC opinion. The health groups did not want to jeopardize the good will of radio and television stations, on which they are dependent for free fund-raising announcements.

John Banzhaf, in the meantime, had quit his New York law firm. Shortly after the FCC ruling, he had been told by one of his senior partners that one of their clients was Philip Morris. This fact seemed unimportant at the time, since Banzhaf had no idea of carrying on an antismoking crusade himself. He hoped that one of the health groups would take up the cause. But to his surprise, as time passed, he was unable to convince any of them to act. By the end of the summer, while the FCC was entertaining petitions to reconsider, he had to make a decision whether he wanted to defend the FCC ruling or remain in the good graces of his law firm, which by now considered his extracurricular activities a definite liability. He decided to quit and organize a defense for the FCC ruling. But before he did so, he telephoned Dr. Donald T. Frederickson, then director of smoking-withdrawal clinics in New York City, and asked him to come to his office at night. The two met in Banzhaf's Manhattan office at 11:30 P.M. and worked out a plan to write prominent physicians asking for money and the use of their names to set up a tax-exempt organization to spearhead the antismoking movement.

Then only twenty-seven years old and widely credited for single-handedly securing the FCC ruling, Banzhaf began soliciting money and volunteers from across the country to monitor radio and television stations. His organization, ASH, an acronym for Action on Smoking and Health, won support from a number of noted physicians, including Dr. Paul Dudley White, and such antismoking stalwarts as Maurine Neuberger, Dr. Alton Ochsner, and Dr. Richard H. Overholt. With these and other backers, Banzhaf had enough money to hire legal assistance and set up a one-room office provided by a small anticancer organization named Cancerco.

After the FCC denied the petitions for reconsideration, the National Association of Broadcasters filed an appeal deep in tobacco country, in the U.S. Court of Appeals in Richmond, Virginia, where the industry's case was expected to get a sympathetic hearing. But Banzhaf had already beaten the broadcasters to the draw. He had gone to Washington and filed an appeal himself in the U.S. Court of Appeals in the District of Columbia on the grounds that the FCC had turned down his request for equal time. Actually, his move was a gambit to have the matter considered by a court that would presumably be more sympathetic to the FCC. Banzhaf lost his appeal, but his gamble paid off, and the fears of the health groups proved unfounded. On November 21, 1968, the Court of Appeals came down strong on the side of the FCC, which, it said, could indeed use its fairness doctrine to require free time for antismoking commercials. "The danger cigarettes may pose to health is, among others, a danger to life itself," the Court said. "As the Commission emphasized, it is a danger inherent in the normal use of the product, not one merely associated with its abuse or dependent on intervening fortuitous events. It threatens a substantial body of the population, not merely a peculiarly susceptible fringe group. Moreover, the danger, though not established beyond all doubt, is documented by a compelling cumulation of statistical evidence."

The cigarette-manufacturers then asked the Supreme Court to review their case. (The high court turned down the request, leaving the appeals court decision standing.) While the question was hanging, the U.S. Public Health Service and numerous health organizations prepared TV and radio spots condemning cigarettes. For example, one series featured romantic couples dining by candlelight, picnicking, and so on, while in the background violins were playing *Smoke Gets in Your Eyes*—and a voice was saying, "Cigarette smoke contains carbon monoxide, formaldehyde, benzopyrene, hydrogen cyanide. It has been related to increased rates of lung cancer, coronary heart disease, peptic ulcers, emphysema. Heavy cigarette-smokers lose about one minute of life for every minute they smoke. So why are these people laughing?" And again: The camera visits the home of William Talman, Perry Mason's late TV courtroom foil. Talman is dying at the age of 53 of lung cancer. He has only six weeks to live. We are shown his handsome sons, wife, and daughters, including little Susan on a tricycle. Then we see Talman himself, gaunt and obviously sedated. "I have lung cancer," he says. "Take some advice about smoking and losing from someone who's been doing both for years. If you haven't smoked, don't start. If you do smoke—quit. Don't be a loser."

Those were but two of the antismoking messages being given tens of millions of dollars' worth of free TV broadcast time—thanks to John Banzhaf and the FCC. The American Cancer Society reported that in the three and one-half years before the FCC applied its fairness doctrine to cigarette ads, it distributed a total of 982 prerecorded antismoking "commercials" for radio and television. In the eight months after the FCC's decisions, the Society distributed 4,723 such commercials. Banzhaf had patients at smoking-withdrawal clinics (by now numerous across the country, as people reacted wth alarm to the new campaign) monitoring broadcasts. ASH filed numerous complaints for violations of the FCC ruling on the basis of these patients' reports and, according to Banzhaf, forced NBC into cutting short four prime-time shows for antismoking spots.

While much has been made of the "David and Goliath" nature of the Banzhaf story, he has done well in worldly terms. When things began to go his way on the bureaucratic front, Banzhaf moved to Washington "to be near the action" and eventually moved into a posh condominium where many prominent Washingtonians, including the Hubert H. Humphreys, resided. He began teaching law at George Washington University law school in 1968. There, out of a tiny third-floor office, he operates two antitobacco outfits, ASH and LASH (the latter stands for Legislative Action on Smoking and Health). He is said to earn about $35,000 a year in combined income from the university and the $20,000 a year he receives from ASH.

Banzhaf's love of publicity has not always gone down well, even with his students and supporters. When he and some student assistants went about Capitol Hill distributing LASHtrays, an ashtray topped by a plastic model of the lungs, one of which turns black if cigarette smoke is puffed up it, the press was alerted beforehand to the stunt. Even friendly congressmen failed to appreciate it.

In testifying before congressional committees, Banzhaf's hyperbole sometimes provides ammunition for his opponents. But in his own defense he has said: "Some people feel you should pick the most important problem. And if I had to rank them on a scale I would certainly put smoking below such things as the war in Vietnam or the racial issue."

Whatever is said about the continuing activities of Banzhaf and his Bandits (as his student teams have inevitably been labeled, in echo of Nader and his Raiders), most observers agree that the dramatic entrance of the Federal Communications Commission into the smoking controversy was probably the most important single event during the three-year moratorium on requiring health warnings in cigarette advertisements imposed by Congress on the Federal Trade Commission. That scarcely any of those who have taken up the cudgels for or against Banzhaf, the young man solely and directly responsible for the FCC's startling action, can be called *objective* observers is not surprising. In cigarette country, there are few such creatures.

♠ 12

The *True* Incident

THINGS HAD NOT been going too well for the cigarette-manufacturers on the publicity front up to January, 1968. Then they received a windfall—or so at first it seemed. An article appeared in the popular and widely read *True* magazine under the title: "To Smoke or Not to Smoke— That Is *Still* the Question," wherein the author, free-lance writer Stanley Frank, claimed to have found contradictions and inconsistencies in the evidence against smoking. He concluded that the "hazards of cigarette smoking may not be so real as we have been led to believe."

"Are cigarettes really 'hazardous to your health' like the package says? Nobody knows," Frank wrote. He continued: "In any case, Americans are smoking more than ever and, curiously, worrying less. When the Surgeon General of the United States issued his report in January, 1964, indicating cigarettes as the chief cause of lung cancer, it figured that smoking would decline, tobacco prices would drop and cigarette company stocks would do poorly on the exchanges." None of this happened, said the writer for *True*. There was no question which side of the smoking question the article took: "Statistics alone link cigarettes with lung cancer, a correlation that is not accepted as scientific proof of the cause and effect. This was admitted in the opening report by the Surgeon General's Committee: 'The Committee was aware that the mere establishment of a statistical correlation between the use of tobacco and a disease is not enough. The causal significance of the use of tobacco in relation to the disease is the crucial question.' "

A second major theme in the article was that there were inconsistencies in the evidence linking cigarette-smoking to lung cancer. After conceding that statistics on mortality rates "seem to indicate that cigarettes were a menace," the author then said:

> However, it is difficult to understand Doctor Terry's abrupt dismissal of other possible causes of lung cancer. Scores of surveys have shown that the mortality from the disease in rural areas is less than half the rate in urban communities, for smokers as well as nonsmokers. Many experts attribute this variation to air pollution in industrial centers, and it hardly is a new theory. In 1775 a London surgeon, Percivall Pott, reported a high incidence of cancer among chimney sweeps. In recent years campaigns to reduce air pollution have been spurred by the strong suspicion that components in coal and gas fumes are cancer-inducing agents. Experiments with animals also suggest that the overcrowding typical of living conditions in cities produces stresses that contribute to cancer.

Frank also found it odd that, while there had been a tremendous increase in women smokers, lung cancer was rare in women and that their death rate from that cause had remained "almost steady." When lung cancer appears, the author said, in the overwhelming majority of cases it is in the lower part of the lung, which is never reached by smoke. Also, he said, most heavy smokers do not contract lung cancer, and a minority who do not smoke also get the disease. If smoking causes cancer, he reasoned, heavy smokers should contract it earlier than nonsmokers, and they don't. To bolster his critique of the Surgeon General's Advisory Committee Report, the writer also said there was more benzopyrene, a cancer-inducing agent, in cigar and pipe smoke than in cigarettes, and yet cigars and pipes were said to be safer than cigarettes. The article asserted that since 1914, cigarette consumption in the United States had increased two-hundred-fold, but the incidence of lung cancer had not increased nearly that much despite better diagnostic methods and a greater awareness of the disease. The mortality rate of 26.6 per 100,000 population would be vastly greater if cigarettes were guilty as charged. "Surprisingly, 39 of the 49 medical authorities and statisticians who testified [at congressional hearings concerning legislation] disagreed vigorously with the report and charged its findings were distorted. Only two of the dissenting experts were connected with the tobacco industry." The article concluded, "At the moment, all we can say for sure is that the cause of cancer isn't known and that there is absolutely no proof that smoking causes human cancer."

The article couldn't have been written better if it had been written by the industry. Two months later, on March 3, 1968, an article entitled "Cigarette Cancer Link Is Bunk," written by Charles Golden, appeared in the *National Enquirer*. The conclusions reached in the *Enquirer* article were identical to those of the *True* article.

But there was more to the story. Both stories.

On March 27, Senator Warren G. Magnuson told the Senate that he and some of his colleagues had received inquiries from their constituents about the Frank article. "Large numbers of reprints of this article have been sent all over the country," he said, "to physicians, lawyers, civic leaders, and other citizens. The note accompanying these reprints gave the impression that the mailing came from the editors of *True* magazine." The Senator went on to say, "My curiosity was aroused by this article, and on March 13, 1968, I asked the Surgeon General to have it reviewed for me."

Senator Magnuson wasn't the only curious one. John Banzhaf was curious, too. He decided to check on the identity of writer Stanley Frank and discovered that he worked for Hill and Knowlton, the public relations firm that had been on a retainer to the Tobacco Institute since 1963. (Although not registered as lobbyists, Hill and Knowlton represent the Washington interests of firms estimated to account for some 10 per cent of the nation's gross product.) On a tip from Banzhaf, the *Wall Street Journal* looked into the situation. On March 21, the *Journal* published a story headlined "Prosmoking Articles Aren't Necessarily All That They Seem to Be," written by Ronald Kessler. It revealed that copies of the *True* article sent out to opinion leaders—slightly more than 600,000 copies in all—were sent not by the magazine but by Tide rock Corporation, a second public relations firm hired by the Tobacco Institute in the fall of 1967, and that the same Stanley Frank later rewrote his original article under the pseudonym of Charles Golden for the *National Enquirer*. The by-line read "Charles Golden," but Nat Chrzan, editor of the *Enquirer,* said the author was Frank. "Charles Golden doesn't exist," Mr. Chrzan told the *Journal* reporter. "It's all perfectly legal." Frank at first flatly denied authorship of the *Enquirer* story, Ronald Kessler reported, but a week later he conceded that he had written it. "You've got me on that one," he said. As to the *True* article, according to Kessler, "Frank said he submitted it last April, while he was a free-lance writer, whereas he didn't join the public relations agency until October."

A similar dispute had arisen early the previous year when a book, *It Is Safe to Smoke,* was published by Hawthorn Books, New York. The book concluded that it was "safer" to smoke cigarettes having charcoal filters such as Liggett & Myers's Lark. Some industry sources said the book amounted almost to a commercial for Lark. Liggett & Myers denied that it had subsidized the book, but Hawthorn agreed to discontinue sales after the Federal Trade Commission began investigating the advertising for it.

The FTC, acting on a complaint from Banzhaf, also looked into the *True* story. An inquiry revealed that in March, 1967, Douglas Kennedy, then editor of *True,* and Joseph Field, a public-relations man retained by Brown & Williamson, became interested in doing an article that would show the tobacco industry's side of the smoking-and-health controversy. In an interview with an FTC investigator, Kennedy characterized himself as a heavy smoker who felt that the smoking-cancer relationship was just propaganda and wanted to have an article on the subject in *True.* To the same interviewer, Joseph Field stated that he had been on a retainer by Brown & Williamson for about two years prior to the *True* article and that, before and after the *True* article, he had sought out other national magazines to do an article on the tobacco industry's side of smoking.

Stanley Frank, then a free-lance writer, was approached by Kennedy and later by Field to draft an outline of an article written along the lines they wanted. Prior to that, Frank had written twenty articles for *True,* all but two or three of which were in the sports field. Since at that point there was no formal commitment that the finished article would be published in *True,* Field reported to the Commission investigator that he paid Stanley Frank $500 to develop the article and that he, Field, had received prior approval and reimbursement for the $500 payment to Frank from Brown & Williamson. The FTC inquiry disclosed that Field introduced Frank to an attorney retained by another tobacco company, who supplied Frank with the materials used in writing the *True* article. Field wrote this attorney, stating, "many thanks for your help in development of this meaningful and impressive story for 'our side.' " A draft outline of the article was submitted to *True* and to Field on April 5, 1967. The following week, Frank was given authority to write the article. It was then circulated among four editors, three of whom gave favorable responses. One of them nevertheless commented, "Andy and Jack [the other approving members of the board], smokers, are comforted and think this is great. I find it completely biased and if actually not hogwash, pretty damn misleading." The fourth member of the editorial board, who later became editor of *True,* was against accepting the article. According to the FTC report, sent to Congress in 1968, the dissenting editor expressed his view in these words: "If our old friend . . . had written this long, sob-sister plea for the tobacco industry I could at least understand his motives, but coming from Stanley Frank, a man who has spent many more years in baseball dugouts than in laboratories, I am at a loss. . . . Let's really face it: what's wrong here is that our writer didn't go out like a good reporter and do his legwork and his homework. The result is the purest trash—dated, biased and without present justification."

Frank received $500 from *True.* He later received additional payments of $1,250 for the article and a $250 bonus due to the article's being featured on the cover of the January issue.

Once the article was accepted in *True,* extensive preparations were made to advertise it and to mail reprints. Such preparations began at least as early as October, 1967. On December 14 and 15, 1967, advertisements of the article were run in some sixty-three newspapers throughout the country. These advertisements contained such excerpts from the article as "at the moment, all we can say for sure is . . . there is absolutely no proof that smoking causes human cancer." They did not disclose that a public-relations man for a tobacco company compensated the author for the article. They did not disclose who paid for the ads.

The commission's inquiry revealed that although the advertising was placed by Ted Barash and Company, the advertising firm for *True* magazine, the format of the ad contained suggestions by Joe Field, and the $67,146.68 bill for the advertising was paid by Tiderock. Tiderock was reimbursed for the cost of the advertising by Brown & Williamson, Philip Morris, and R. J. Reynolds, all members of the Tobacco Institute.

Plans to distribute reprints of the *True* article were revealed in a letter from Joe Field to the Tiderock Corporation dated October 27, 1967. The Tobacco Institute's role in planning the reprint can be judged from a memorandum that it sent to the tobacco companies stating, "[w]e are preparing a proposal for reprint distribution." At the instigation of the Institute, Tiderock directed the art work, setting of type, printing and shipping operations for 607,934 reprints to be purchased from Fawcett Publications, the publisher of *True*. The Barash agency prepared the layout of the eight-page reprint, for which it received $1,599.75 from Tiderock. Tiderock also ordered and paid for 554,000 copies of a message to be used to transmit the reprints. This message stated: "As a leader in your profession and community, you will be interested in reading this story from the January issue of *TRUE* Magazine about one of today's controversial issues—THE EDITORS."

Douglas Kennedy told the commission investigator that

as editor he had authority to grant permission for reprints of an article appearing in *True*. He indicated that he had no knowledge that the reprints would be mailed without identifying the sender. However, a letter was uncovered from the Barash agency dated December 26, 1967, notifying Kennedy of an intention to use the noted transmittal message in connection with the mailing of the reprints.

To what extent were the reprints disseminated? Tiderock retained R. L. Polk & Co., a Detroit, Michigan, mailing house, to distribute 414,820 of the 607,934 reprints purchased. These were mailed with the transmittal message and the address of the mailing house on the envelope. Mailing lists were obtained to gain the widest distribution possible. Even in obtaining mailing lists from the American Medical Association, any connection with the tobacco industry was not disclosed: Although Tiderock was administering and guiding all phases of the reprint distribution, it had the Barash agency address a letter to the AMA seeking a mailing list ostensibly for the purpose of gaining greater circulation for *True*.

This was the distribution of individuals receiving the reprint, according to the FTC:

Medical field	184,647
Communications field	7,295
Biological scientists	41,055
Educators	18,819
Government officials (including 50 governors, 100 senators, 432 representatives)	10,142
Security analysts	10,173
Other opinion leaders (lawyers, Junior Chamber of Commerce members)	123,779
	414,820*

* *The report is as it went to Congress. Alert readers will note that the total is incorrect.*

In addition to the mailing of the reprints, bulk shipments without the transmittal message were sent to two
tobacco trade groups, the National Association of Tobacco
Distributors and the Tobacco Growers Information Committee. Four tobacco companies—Lorillard, R. J. Reynolds, Brown & Williamson, and Philip Morris—obtained
approximately 100,000 reprints from Tiderock to send to
their stockholders, employees, and sales forces. Reprints
were also purchased directly from Fawcett Publications
in the following amounts:

American Tobacco	200,000
Philip Morris	65,100
R. J. Reynolds	135,000

Altogether, more than 1 million reprints were mailed
out by tobacco interests. The cost of this project was as
follows:

Ted Barash	Art work and layout	$ 1,599.75
Fawcett Publications	Printing of article	19,450.70
R. L. Polk	Mailing	82,363.00
National Association of Tobacco Distributors	Mailing	320.52
Freight	Leftover reprints mailed to Tiderock	69.80
Tobacco Growers Information Commission	Mailing	3,825.00
		$107,628.77

When the advertising costs are added to the above amount,
the *True* magazine article promotional campaign cost the
Tobacco Institute and members at least $175,000

The commission inquiry into the article entitled "Cigarette Cancer Link Is Bunk," which appeared in the *Na-*

tional Enquirer, disclosed that the editor of the *Enquirer* read the *True* article and "wanted to present the other side of the cigarette cancer scare" in his newspaper. He attempted to secure a reprint from *True* but was turned down by Douglas Kennedy. Stanley Frank, who at this time was an employee of Hill and Knowlton, was contacted and persuaded to write an article for the *Enquirer.* The name "Charles Golden" was the normal house by-line used by the *Enquirer* to keep the identity of the author confidential. Nat Chrzan, the *Enquirer* editor, emphatically stated to a commission investigator that he received no compensation for having the article in the *Enquirer.*

Surgeon General William H. Stewart, meantime, had submitted comments on the articles to Senator Magnuson. According to the Public Health Service, the *True* article conformed to a pattern of attack on Surgeon General Luther L. Terry and his advisory committee on smoking and health, Stewart said. Dr. Terry had said three years before that such attacks "are repetitious and cleverly manipulated in a continuing program to shake public confidence in the Report." Taking up Frank's first point, that cigarettes really are not hazardous to health and that Americans are smoking as much as ever, the Public Health Service chief and spokesman said that smoking is a hazard to health is known by practically everybody who has studied the subject and that

> although total cigarette consumption increases as population increases, the rate of growth of the habit has been seriously curtailed since the evidence on the effects of smoking was first brought to the public's attention in 1953. If the average annual rate of increase in per capita consumption of cigarettes that existed from 1947 to 1953 had continued through 1966, the total U.S. consumption of cigarettes

would have been over 700 billion in 1966. Instead, the Department of Agriculture reported an actual figure of 541 billion for that year, a reduction of nearly one-fourth over what might have been expected. In all of the 11 years from 1955 to 1966, the number of adult cigarette smokers increased by one-sixth, from about 42 million to about 49 million. During this same time, the number of successful ex-smokers more than doubled, from less than 8 million to about 19 million. Moreover, Americans continue to give up smoking cigarettes at the rate of about one million a year.

Are Americans worrying less? The Public Health Service head replied: "The fact that filter cigarettes account for about 70 per cent of all cigarettes now sold in the United States, compared to approximately 9 per cent sold in 1954, suggests that smokers who are unable or unwilling to give up smoking are using filters in the expectation that they are thereby reducing their exposure to the harmful ingredients in tobacco smoke."

"When Mr. Frank refers to 'conclusions reached by Dr. Terry' and 'Dr. Terry's abrupt dismissal of other possible causes of lung cancer,' as he does later in the article," the Public Health Service chief claimed,

he distorts the role of the Surgeon General in the preparation of his study. The Report was the work of an Advisory Committee of ten men, drawn from a list of 150 scientists and physicians representing all the pertinent scientific disciplines. The tobacco industry, among other groups and organizations, was given full opportunity to veto any of the names on the list, no reasons being required. . . .

Assuming that the evidence in the Surgeon General's Report were only statistical, which it clearly is not, the case against cigarettes would still be strong enough to act on. Statistics have been used and are essential in every branch of medical science. The distinguished scientist, Warren

Weaver, said in *Science Magazine* that "it is shocking that various groups, in order to shake public confidence in statements which they find uncomfortable, are taking the position that it is silly to be impressed by evidence that is 'only statistical.'"

Furthermore, the committee did *not* say cigarette-smoking was the *only* cause of lung cancer, but that it was the principal cause, Stewart pointed out. He added: "Air pollution is apparently a risk factor since studies have shown that lung cancer occurs more frequently among people who live in cities than among those who live in the country. This was stated in the Report. However, this increase is not nearly as significant as that existing between smokers and nonsmokers. In Iceland, which has some of the purest air in Europe, lung cancer, once a rare disease, has risen with the increase in cigarette smoking."

Moreover, "In his discussion of causes of lung cancer, it is not clear why the author cites the report in 1775 of Percivall Pott on the incidence of cancer among chimney sweeps. It was not lung cancer that was involved but cancer of the scrotum, and it had nothing to do with air pollution."

The Surgeon General challenged a number of statements in the article, mainly concerned with lung cancer, which he said were inaccurate. As far as lung cancer in women was concerned, he said, the lung cancer death rate for women has increased more than 50 per cent in the past fourteen years, and 400 per cent since 1930. According to the best evidence, all cigarette-smokers don't get lung cancer because some smokers are more susceptible than others, some may not have smoked long enough to develop the disease, and other smokers die of other causes before they are stricken. Cigarette-smokers develop a different kind of lung cancer from that afflicting lung-cancer victims who do not smoke. By far the most common lung cancer—bronchogenic or squamos-cell carcinoma—occurs almost entirely among cigarette-smokers and rarely in those who have never smoked. Studies have shown a clear relationship between the amount of cigarettes smoked and the risk of dying from lung cancer. In comparison with nonsmokers, the average male smokers of cigarettes have approximately a nine-to-ten-fold risk of dying of lung cancer, and heavy smokers at least a twenty-fold risk, he stated. As to benzo-pyrene in cigar and pipe smoke, the degree of inhalation is important to the risk factor, and it seems clear that the smoke from cigars and pipes is rarely inhaled.

With reference to the 1965 congressional hearings, Stewart said:

> It is no reflection on the professional integrity of the dissent-ing experts to point out that in response to a questionnaire later sent to them by Senator Daniel B. Brewster of Mary-land, all indicated that they appeared at the request of the tobacco industry and that five of them indicated they received payment from tobacco industry representatives for their testimony and the time spent in preparing it. It should also be pointed out that while the dissenting experts spoke for a small minority, and usually for themselves alone, other witnesses, speaking for the major professional groups and voluntary health organizations, clearly represented the con-sensus of medical thinking throughout the United States.

The American Cancer Society, commenting on the *True* article, reviewed the evidence against smoking and mentioned the work of Dr. Oscar Auerbach, whose experi-ments with dogs would become a point of controversy a couple of years later:

In a series of biological—not "statistical"—experiments, Dr. Auerbach has shown that dogs in his laboratory which have been taught to smoke in roughly human-fashion have demonstrated an appalling knack for the lung disease which in human beings would be termed "emphysema"; a disease which in the decade from 1953 to 1963 increased in America some five-fold times. Furthermore, Dr. Auerbach reported that "histologic changes in bronchial epithelium, including dysplastic lesions, can be produced experimentally in animals exposed to cigarette smoke."

At first, the American Cancer Society stated, it felt it best to ignore *True's* article. "Given the irresponsibility of the research, its ambiguous status as a 'fact acticle,' and its fantastically wide reprint distribution . . . the Society felt the need to reply and to raise the question as to the wisdom and morality of the distribution of this misleading article from a carefully concealed tobacco industry source."

The American Cancer Society then asked this question —the real kicker. "Does this indicate that the Tobacco Institute, which has usually been quite candid, now feels guilty or is it running scared?" A lot of people by now were beginning to wonder.

♦ 13

1969–70: Showdown in Washington

NOBODY IN CONGRESS has ever proposed an outright ban on the sale of cigarettes; the painful experience of Prohibition is still too close for that. But by 1969 the stage had been set for a showdown over cigarette advertising and promotion. Should an industry be at liberty to promote a product millions of Americans wanted even if it endangered life? What was the responsibility of industry? What restrictive measures, if any, should the government take?

Opinions differed as to the economic effects of an advertising blackout on television. Antismoking advocates argued that too much had been said about the economics of the industry and too little about the economic losses from disease and death due to smoking. At a time when Americans generally were enjoying expanded personal liberties, these questions went to the heart of the concept of freedom.

In the broadest and most direct campaign ever made against a legally marketable product, the U.S. Government was steadily increasing its efforts to discourage the sale of cigarettes. Post Office trucks carried posters: "100,000 Doctors Have Quit Smoking." The Surgeon General continued to release increasingly damning reports about the health effects of smoking. Dr. Daniel Horn, director of the National Clearinghouse for Smoking and Health, was urging doctors to deliver antismoking appeals to patients in their offices. His Clearinghouse, called the "Smokehouse" by staffers, was churning out antismoking tracts for civic groups and had started several local anti-cigarette projects. At Bakersfield, California, for example, a group of teenagers was given $52,000 plus professional assistance in preparing commercials, posters, and bumper stickers ("Smoke, Choke, Croak" was one of their inspirations).

Although it was directed from Washington, the anti-smoking campaign had caught on around the country. Other communities were enrolled. In the town of Green-field, Iowa, some 376 smokers threw their cigarettes into a bonfire and signed no-smoking pledges to publicize *Cold Turkey,* a Dick Van Dyke movie involving the trials of giving up cigarettes that was being filmed in the town at the time. Turlock, California, held a month-long anti-smoking drive and put up billboards on the roads leading into town that read "End Emphysema . . . Cut Coronaries . . . Clean the Air," and "Please Don't Smoke. We're Trying to Quit." A number of celebrities were taking part in public campaigns against smoking. Movie actor Tony Curtis had become head of an American Cancer Society campaign called I.Q. (for "I Quit") that passed out lapel buttons and dispatched public speakers around the coun-try to spread the word. Doris Day, Debbie Reynolds, and Lawrence Welk refused to allow tobacco companies to sponsor their TV shows. At least two ad agencies—Ogilvy & Mather and Doyle Dane Bernbach—and a few radio and television stations would not accept cigarette business. The antismoking campaign had become something of a chil-dren's crusade, too. Youngsters, fresh from seeing antismoking commercials on television, were putting pressure on their parents to kick the habit.

A minor industry had sprung up to cater to the millions of smokers who wanted to quit. Nikoban, Bantron, and other trade-named aids were enjoying a brisk sale. To respond to a need for help in breaking the habit, withdrawal clinics had also sprung up across the country. Many of the antismoking clinics operated by health agencies and religious groups were offering their services free. Among the oldest of these was the five-day program offered by the Seventh Day Adventist Church, in which, to open each session, smokers began by chanting "I choose not to smoke." The free programs often featured gruesome films of lung-cancer surgery, and smokers were enjoined to eat well-balanced meals, go on brisk walks, and pray for strength each day. A growing demand for antismoking help had also attracted enterprising businessmen to the clinic idea. In Hollywood, for example, actor Paul Newman and his wife, Joanne Woodward, were among the graduates of Sunset Boulevard's "Smoking Control Center," just one of several $125-a-course clinics to have opened in the Los Angeles area. Smoke Watchers International was franchising clinics at the rate of thirty a week from California to New York. Clinic directors were ex-smokers who agreed to run three sessions a week and pay the company 20 per cent of each $30,000 they made and 10 per cent of earnings thereafter. Smokers paid $3 to join and $2 per session for an average of twelve weeks. Smoke Watchers was set up on the group-therapy principle. Members shared their smoking trials and tribulations with each other and set a goal for the number of cigarettes they would give up every week. Smokers were advised to give up "habit" cigarettes first and work later on the problem of cigarettes they smoked for "emotional" reasons. One of the toughest in the latter category, smokers were warned, was the "after-sex" cigarette. Sleep immediately after intercourse was recommended. Despite these efforts, the Department of Health, Education, and Welfare estimated that only 45 per cent of the people who really wanted to quit did so for as long as three weeks. Less than half of those were able to abstain for a full year.

And yet Americans were undoubtedly losing some of their taste for smoking. Opinion pollster Louis Harris reported that in four years the smoking population had declined from 47 per cent to 42 per cent of those over twenty-one. One reason clearly was that, in the same period, the number of Americans who believed smoking was a "major cause" of lung cancer had risen from 40 to 49 per cent. By a ratio of five to four, Harris found, Americans favored restrictions on TV and radio ads for cigarettes.

The smoking controversy had its share of ironies. The Public Health Service was encouraging smokers to use filter cigarettes, while the Federal Trade Commission would not permit cigarette advertising even to hint that filter-tip cigarettes were safer. And even while the Department of Health, Education, and Welfare was spending $2.1 million a year to educate the public to the dangers of smoking, the Department of Agriculture was paying out more than twice that every year in price supports to tobacco farmers. To boost tobacco exports, which were making a $500-million-a-year contribution to the U.S. balance of payments, the Department of Agriculture was also promoting overseas sales. Moreover, the tobacco industry was receiving a hidden subsidy granted to only one other crop (cotton) of about $3 million a year in the form of voluntary grading of tobacco leaf by the Department of Agriculture.

This official schizophrenia was characterized by Senator John J. Williams (R., Delaware) as an "absurdity." On the floor of the Senate, in early 1969, Williams asked the question: "Why spend millions emphasizing the danger of tobacco while at the same time spending more millions to subsidize the production?" In the previous three years, Williams reported, the Department of Agriculture's Commodity Credit Corporation had spent or lost $71.2 million, $61.5 million of which was to subsidize the export of this product and its sales in foreign countries, and $9.7 million of which represented a direct loss in its price-support operations. "Another $69.3 million worth of tobacco was disposed as foreign aid under Public Law 480," Williams said. "Under this program the tobacco is sold for local—soft—currencies which cannot be converted into dollars. Such sales for soft currencies ultimately represent a near 100 per cent loss for taxpayers." This use of tobacco under Public Law 480, better known as the Food for Peace program, seemed particularly ironic. Whatever other virtues it has been thought to have, tobacco has never been considered a food.

A year before, Senator Frank E. Moss, one of the leading antismoking members of Congress, had written then Agriculture Secretary Orville Freeman to ask whether his department had given any consideration to the possibility that tobacco-growers might turn their land to other crops. To this query, Freeman replied:

We know of no commodities in short supply to which the growers could turn if the demand for tobacco were eliminated. In some areas they would turn to feed grains and soybeans and other crops in ample or excess supply. However, any substantial decline in tobacco production would not only have a serious economic impact but would create sociological problems as the small farms which now support a family and provide employment for the family would be unable to do so. I believe the majority of the tobacco growers, particularly in hilly and mountainous sections of the country, would be forced to discontinue farming as a way of life and thus the problem of migration from the farm to the already crowded cities would be accelerated.

This alarming picture—of deserted farms, silent factories, out-of-work Negro field hands moving to the North, where they would further swell the ghettos and relief rolls —was just the sort of specter the tobacco industry itself was not loath to raise.

Two federal agencies had served notice that they intended to cut deeper into cigarette sales if the legislative ban on regulations was allowed to expire. Sales had declined from 572.6 billion cigarettes in 1967 to 571.7 billion in 1968. This seemed like a small reduction. But it was disturbing to an industry geared, before the 1964 Surgeon General's Advisory Committee Report, to steady growth. In 1968, per capita consumption of cigarettes among American adults dropped from 210 packs to 205. Over-all industry profits remained high, but only because the tobacco men had been able to step up exports and sales of nontobacco items. The Federal Communications Commission had proposed to ban all cigarette commercials from the airwaves. In March, the Federal Trade Commission announced the results of tests that showed that yields of both tar and nicotine had increased during the previous four months in twenty-seven varieties of cigarettes while decreasing in only one. After FTC machines puffed two packs of each of 121 domestic varieties purchased in fifty cities, the FTC compared the results with those obtained when the same 121 varieties were tested four months earlier. Senator Frank E. Moss, who headed the Senate Commerce subcommittee on consumer affairs, termed the FTC findings "at best discouraging and, at worst, sinister."

The Tobacco Institute countered with the allegation that, because of "recognized deficiencies" in the FTC's "testing and reporting," the burden was on the commission "to justify its report." But Senator Moss raised the possibility that the cigarette companies had deliberately stepped up the nicotine content because "nicotine is closely related to the addictive or habituating quality of cigarette smoking." In a Senate speech, Moss said, "Again, we can only conclude that the cigarette industry is not interested in competing to market less hazardous cigarettes, an unhappy reflection of its sense of social responsibility." He said that the industry was not entitled to an extension of legislation —advocated by tobacco-state congressmen—that would "place a straitjacket" on possible efforts by the FTC to require a health warning in cigarette advertising and by the FCC to ban all cigarette advertising on television and radio.

Both the FCC and the FTC were urging that the warning on cigarette packs be strengthened to read "Warning: Cigarette Smoking is Dangerous to Health and May Cause Death from Cancer and Other Diseases," and both agencies wanted this warning included in all cigarette advertisements and commercials. The words "death" and "cancer" made the tobacco people extremely uncomfortable.

One strong reason why the industry was reluctant to concede a link between smoking and disease was its fear of damage suits. Some seventy or eighty such suits (similar to the *Lartigue* case) had been brought in recent years (to date, including *Lartigue,* only seven have gone to trial). No tobacco company had ever lost a case. There had been no known out-of-court settlements. In one case, involving a lung-cancer victim, Edwin L. Green, a Florida jury ordered American Tobacco to pay damages, but in 1969, American won a reversal from a U.S. Court of Appeals.

The package label makes it more difficult, but not impossible, for anyone to sue for breach of warranty. The consumer has been warned; he now smokes at his own risk.

The FCC's proposed ban on radio and television commercials, approved in February, 1969, by six of the seven commissioners, held that cigarette-smoking was a "most serious, unique danger to public health," and concluded that "it would thus appear wholly at odds with the public interest for broadcasters to present advertising promoting the consumption of the product posing this unique danger —a danger measured in terms of an epidemic of deaths and disabilities." The FCC stressed that its action was "limited to the unique situation and product, that we are unaware of any other product commercials calling for such action, and expressly disclaim any intention to proceed against other product commercials." But dissenting Commissioner James J. Wadsworth suggested that advertising for other products might one day be ordered off the air and called the majority's decision "unreasonable and arbitrary."

Predictably, this was also the reaction of both the tobacco and broadcast industries. Cigarette companies had become the largest single product-advertisers on television, accounting for about 8 per cent of its advertising time. The automobile industry, second largest advertiser, took one-third less time. In reaction to the FCC proposed ban, Vincent T. Wasilewski, president of the National Association of Broadcasters, said: "Not only do we deplore the assumption of such power, but we deny that such power exists." The Tobacco Institute called the FCC decision "arbitrary in the extreme" and "an obvious threat to usurp the congressional function."

Despite these reactions, there were hints that those old allies, the manufacturers and the broadcasters, were getting ready to make some concession in return for immunity from further federal regulation. Robert MacNeil, in his 1968 book about television, *People Machine* (New York: Harper & Row, 1968), wrote that "a ban on cigarette advertising is anticipated in the industry. In fact, CBS has budgeted for 1969 on the assumption that the nineteen per cent of its revenues attributed to cigarette advertising would be missing. The network feels that either the Government will ban such commercials or the network will feel morally obliged to do so itself." CBS denied the nineteen per cent figure. Although they would not confirm the reports, other networks were believed to have similar contingency plans in the event of an anticipated loss of cigarette revenue.

It had not escaped the attention of either the broadcasters or tobacco men that dropping of cigarette commercials would, in all probability, free broadcasters from the obligation to carry public-service antismoking messages. The money saved could be used by the tobacco companies in different ways—to encourage programs of corporate diversification already under way, to add product lines, and in other ways to hedge against possible further declines in product sales. Lorillard had merged with Loew's, a hotel and movie chain. The American Tobacco Company, which had once boasted "Tobacco is Our Middle Name," had decided to change its name to American Brands, Incorporated. Reflecting the trend, Reynolds also dropped "tobacco" from its name. In addition to producing Pall Mall, Tareyton, Lucky Strike, and Silva Thins, American was producing Mott's apple sauce, Sunshine biscuits, and Jim Beam Kentucky bourbon. Reynolds, Philip Morris, and Liggett & Myers had all moved into noncigarette businesses. Some stock-market analysts thought the earnings of cigarette-manufacturers might even get a short-term fillip if companies did not plow all their TV money into other media. After a report to that effect in mid-December, 1968, by the Wall Street brokerage house Smith, Barney & Company, prices of tobacco stocks picked up. And when the FCC's proposed ban was announced in February, 1969, tobacco stocks rose on the New York Exchange.

But the industry, speaking through its mouthpiece, the Tobacco Institute, was sticking to the argument that no scientific case had been made against smoking. The Institute, with offices in a modern office-building on K Street, in downtown Washington, a staff of about twenty-five, including economists, librarians, statisticians, and public-relations experts, was now headed by Earle Clements, the former congressman who, as a lobbyist, had led the successful fight on the Hill in 1964 and 1965. The Institute was supported by contributions from member companies, but it declined to reveal its budget. The industry had also set up the Council for Tobacco Research—U.S.A., which had spent boasted "millions" to research a "scientific understanding of the actual facts, whatever these facts turn out to be."

A news release from the Council, widely advertised in the newspapers by the Institute under the caption "How much is known about smoking and health?" was that there were other causes of cancer, that statistical associations between smoking and lung cancer do not prove a causal relationship, and that effective tests of the real relationship had yet to be devised. William Kloepfer, Jr., a former newspaperman who was with the drug industry before joining the Tobacco Institute as chief of public relations, took the line that the causal relationship between smoking and the two dozen or so diseases with which it has been associated had not been demonstrated, that there were many factors involved, and until their roles were understood, no one could be sure about the role of smoking. This was the gist of a "white paper" entitled "The Cigarette Controversy: Eight Questions and Answers" published by the Council for Tobacco Research shortly before resumption of congressional hearings early in 1969. In full-page ads that ran in major newspapers on February 28, the Tobacco Institute quoted Dr. Clarence Cook Little, the eighty-year-old retired biologist who headed the Tobacco Research Council, as declaring that "there is no demonstrated causal relationship between smoking and any disease." Dr. Cook went on to say: "The gaps in knowledge are so great that those who dogmatically assert otherwise—whether they state that there is or is not such a causal relationship—are premature in judgment. If anything, the pure biological evidence is pointing away from, not toward, the causal hypothesis."

"After 15 years of trying, nobody has induced lung cancer in animals with cigarette smoke," said a full-page ad placed in the *New York Times* by one of the tobacco companies in 1969. "We believe that the anti-cigarette theory is a bum rap." Unfortunately, for the cigarette people, this and similar flat statements appeared just six months before the American Cancer Society announced that experiments by the two well-known scientists, Doctors Oscar Auerbach and E. Cuyler Hammond, showed, among other things, that twelve out of eighty-six beagles trained to smoke had developed lung cancer.

Researchers had long been able to produce skin cancer in mice and other laboratory animals by rubbing their backs with condensed tar distillates of tobacco smoke. In previous work by other experimenters, rodents died after being exposed to cigarette smoke. But previous attempts to reproduce the effects of human smoke in the laboratory had failed because animals could not be taught to inhale.

Then Dr. William G. Cahan of the Sloan-Kettering Institute came up with the answer. He devised an ingenious method of inserting a plastic tube through an opening in beagles' windpipes and pumping in smoke drawn from cigarettes. A curved Teflon tube was held in place by a padded crosspiece snapped to a special leather collar which was, in turn, attached to an apparatus that pumped smoke through the cigarette into the dogs' lungs. The beagles were harnessed in an open box and, after a few weeks of conditioning, began to show signs of addiction.

Dr. Auerbach and his colleagues began to use this technique in the mid-1960's. Their first report on smoking dogs, presented in 1966, showed cell changes in the bronchial linings of all of five animals who smoked for 420 days. These pilot studies had shown that beagles develop such lung diseases as emphysema and pulmonary fibrosis as well as changes that, when examined under a microscope, resembled early cancer. A second experiment was set up in 1967, in which more beagles were to smoke for a longer period of time. In this experiment, it was also hoped that something could be learned about the effectiveness of filters. At a news conference held on February 5, 1970, at the Waldorf-Astoria, following a scientific session of the American Cancer Society, Auerbach and Hammond disclosed that, in addition to inducing lung cancer in the twelve beagles, they had found "dramatic differences in the incidence of malignant tumors in the filter-smoking and non-filter-smoking dogs and that the degree of lung damage progresses with duration of smoking."

Tobacco stocks dropped broadly on this news. But the Tobacco Institute stuck to its guns. It called the Auerbach-Hammond report interesting but said it was impossible to "draw a meaningful parallel between human smoking and dogs subjected to these most stressful conditions." The

Institute later disclosed that the American Cancer Society had three times denied its request for an independent scientific review of the findings. When newly appointed Surgeon General Jesse L. Steinfeld, successor to Doctors Stewart and Terry, was called into the controversy, he said: "If the question at issue is whether human-type lung cancer has been discovered in the lungs of dogs exposed to cigarette smoke, then the answer is yes, in the view of a Public Health Service pathologist with special competence in cancer."

The health debate raged throughout 1969 and 1970. The Tobacco Institute cited surveys showing that smokers are unusually energetic, marry more often, and drink more liquor and black coffee than nonsmokers. Smokers, the Institute concluded, are a "different kind of people" who are perhaps more susceptible to sickness. The tobacco men, in ridiculing the idea that cigarettes alone could be responsible for certain diseases, also argued that much more research would have to be done on such factors as air pollution, urbanization, and the stressful emotional environment that goes with it. Genetic and behavioral factors may be involved in causing disease, they contended.

Indirectly, the American Medical Association helped the industry in propounding this point of view. In a 1968 review of its tobacco research project, the AMA had said that

> the problems related to establishing any kind of cause-and-effect relationship between tobacco use and health are far more complex than had been supposed. The products of tobacco combustion are many and varied. New techniques must be developed for their separation, for their administration, and for their study. In addition, the effects of smoking must be distinguished from the effects of the ever increasing environmental pollution attributable to automobile engines

and industrial wastes. It is evident that we have a long road to travel and that this will be done slowly. Many years may be required to gather sufficient experimental facts and data to clear what is at best a muddied picture.

But medical men also pointed out that the statistics on deaths from lung cancer had reached impressive proportions and were continuing to pile up evidence against smoking. Experiments backed by laboratory experiments, sometimes sponsored by industry, were continuing with mice, dogs, baboons, and other animals. The Arthur D. Little Company of Boston was doing work with chickens that showed that smoke gases temporarily paralyze the tiny, hairlike cilia that normally keep foreign matter out of the lungs. Other studies had identified a number of carcinogens in cigarette smoke.

HEW Secretary Wilbur J. Cohen, in his final report to Congress in early 1969, had stated:

Five years after the American people received their first official warning on smoking and health, cigarette consumption in the United States had dropped by more than one billion cigarettes in 1968. Though we number two million more adults, we have increased evidence that more and more adults are giving up smoking and fewer teenagers are taking it up. Still, smoking, a grave problem in 1964, is graver today. To some extent it can be said that cigarette smoking has cancelled many of the health gains made in recent years. Deaths and disease associated with cigarette smoking continue to rise. In 1964 there were nearly 46,000 deaths from lung cancer; this year it will be over 59,000. Five years ago emphysema and chronic bronchitis killed 20,000 Americans; twice that number will die this year of these respiratory diseases. Cigarette smoking contributes to coronary heart disease: in 1964 there were 545,000 deaths from this disease; in 1969 it is expected to be 590,000. What's more, the nation's workers who smoke cigarettes spend over a third more time away from the job because of illness than those who do not smoke.

The tobacco toll was placed in an even grimmer light by Dr. E. Cuyler Hammond of the American Cancer Society, who suggested that there was a total of about 300,000 cigarette-related deaths a year. A study presented by Dr. Hammond indicated that a man who smokes two packs or more a day at age twenty-five or thirty-five can expect to live 8.3 years less than a nonsmoker at the same age. At age forty-five, the heavy smoker's life expectancy was said to be seven years less; at fifty-five, five years less; and at sixty-five, four years less. Even men smoking fewer than ten cigarettes a day have a life expectancy of 2.8 to 4.6 years shorter than that of nonsmokers. In other words, nonsmokers on the average live four years longer than those who smoke less than a pack a day, and eight years longer than those who smoke two packs or more.

A few weeks before the House Interstate and Foreign Commerce Committee was scheduled to open hearings, a bill was introduced in the House that might have given the casual reader of the *Congressional Record* the idea that tobacco-state legislators had suddenly become deeply concerned about the health hazards of cigarette smoking. "A bill to extend public health protection with respect to cigarette smoking and for other purposes," said the title of H.R. 7177, which declared it to be the policy of Congress "to establish a comprehensive Federal program to deal with cigarette labeling and advertising with respect to any relationship between smoking and health." H.R. 7177 bore the name of all eleven of North Carolina's House delegation. Identical measures were introduced under the sponsorship of congressmen from Virginia,

Maryland, Kentucky, and Florida. What was going on? Had the antismoking commercials of the American Cancer Society suddenly made a hit in Marlboro country? Not exactly. H.R. 7177 and its companion bills were actually intended to prevent strengthening of the warning label and make permanent the ban on state and federal regulation of cigarette advertising, which was due to expire on June 30. Passage of this legislation was the best tobacco interests could have hoped for under the circumstances.

The tobacco lobbyists were busy on Capitol Hill. Earle Clements was now assisted by former North Carolina Congressman Horace R. Kornegay, who had become vice president and counsel at the Tobacco Institute. No sooner had Congress convened than members received a letter from Jack Mills, former executive director of the Republican Campaign Committee, who had also joined the Institute. His letter said that unless the 1965 provisions were extended, "several downtown agencies and every one of the state legislatures will be able to jump in with special regulations of cigarette advertising, and the result will be commercial chaos." He warned that "The tobacco industry, from the grower to the retailer, will suffer greatly."

A number of states were again considering action against cigarette advertising. Interest was running high in California, Massachusetts, Michigan, and New York. In essence, the lobbyists' theme was that if the FCC and the FTC were allowed to ban or control the contents of cigarette advertising, it would set a dangerous precedent for banning or restricting all sorts of other legally sold products. For instance, it was reported that the Liquor Institute was sending a lobbyist around the Hill in support of the tobacco people. The big Washington law firms were active, as always, on behalf of their clients, with Arnold & Porter still representing Philip Morris.

But the industry's elaborate public-relations effort had not been running altogether smoothly. Hill and Knowlton's carefully engineered low-profile approach had been superseded or supplemented, or at any rate had its cover blown by the counterattack that culminated in the *True* magazine affair. Hill and Knowlton found itself embarrassed in that episode, and soon after the particulars were publicized, the agency resigned the Tobacco Institute account. American and Lorillard had quit the Tobacco Institute because of differences over the style and substance of the industry's defense.

On Capitol Hill, opposition to the tobacco interests had grown since 1965, when the controversy had been given its first full airing. Congressmen from tobacco states were staunch in their support of tobacco, of course. But the industry's cause had been damaged by the defeat or retirement of some of its most effective friends, notably former Senator Thruston Morton of Kentucky. Many congressmen were also sensitive to the growing antismoking movement. Bills calling for greater control of advertising had been introduced by fifty-four sponsors in the House. Most of the bills were similar to a measure sponsored by the leading opponent of smoking in the House, California Democrat John E. Moss, who proposed toughening the cigarette-label warning and ordering it in all ads as the FTC had proposed. In addition, Moss would have given the commission power to limit the length of cigarettes. The critics of cigarettes were also excited by the idea that if the 1965 labeling law's pre-emptive clause was permitted to expire, the FTC and the FCC would be free to do almost anything they wanted. No cigarette bills of any kind were pending in the Senate, but Senator Warren G. Magnuson, chairman of the Commerce Committee in 1969 as he had been in 1965, and Utah's Frank E. Moss had girded themselves for a bristling fight. Their tactic was simply to prevent any legislation on the subject to come to the floor. Should they fail, Senator Moss promised to filibuster the legislation to death.

During the first round of hearings on April 15, former Surgeon General Luther Terry, testifying for the Interagency Council on Smoking and Health (a coalition of government agencies and virtually every national health organization except the AMA), said that 45,000 Americans would die prematurely by July "from causes which we believe are connected with cigarette smoking." Surgeon General William Stewart repeated his conviction that "we have established cause and effect in lung cancer. I don't think there is any question about it." He told the House Interstate and Foreign Commerce Committee that he favored more explicit and more broadly applied warning labels rather than a flat ban on broadcast advertising. Even FCC Chairman Rosel Hyde somewhat softened his position and told the House Commerce Committee that he would be willing to forego the ban if Congress ordered health warnings "in every bit of advertising, in print, or radio or television." Speaking in behalf of the cigarette-makers, the Philip Morris board chairman, Joseph F. Cullman III, indicated that few if any manufacturers would be willing to advertise that cigarettes may cause "cancer" and "death."

Cullman chain smoked during his appearance before the House Committee. But, earlier than most, his firm had been diversifying into other consumer products. In the previous decade, Philip Morris had acquired some twenty companies and, in the process, had picked up several well-known brands, among them Clark (chewing gum), Personna (razor blades), SteriSharp (surgical instruments), and Miller High Life (beer). Thanks to these moves and also to Philip Morris's highly successful overseas-expansion program, sales had climbed dramatically, the company's per-share profits had nearly doubled, and earnings were up sharply. As its most recent venture, Philip Morris was going into real estate with a substantial acquisition of land in Southern California.

The tobacco industry won its first legislative skirmish of 1969. Under the leadership of Earle Clements, the tobacco lobby showed that it could still pack enough power to call the turn in the House. By giving in on one point—a strengthened label warning—it won on the most important issue, regulation of advertising: On May 27, the House Committee on Interstate and Foreign Commerce, in executive session, voted twenty-two to five for a stiffer health warning but prohibited regulatory action on cigarette advertising for six years and in other ways generally upheld the *status quo*. One rather nasty shock awaited the tobacco forces.

In the course of their lobbying exercises on behalf of the tobacco interests, the broadcasters had put forward the argument that they were already monitoring and regulating cigarette advertising through the National Association of Broadcasters Television Code Review Board. "The industry recognizes its obligations," NAB President Wasilewski told the House committee. Through the Code, he said, the industry was maintaining a continuing review of cigarette advertising on radio and television. "We believe that self-regulatory efforts have played and are playing a significant role in dealing with the issue, and that the furtherance of such efforts should be encouraged." However, to the surprise of everyone, in mid-June, Representative Brock Adams (D., Washington), one of the five dissenting committee members, turned up some evidence very much to the contrary. It came from deep inside the NAB itself. Warren Braren, former manager of the New York office of the Code Authority, appeared at a special hearing to testify that for years the NAB had been impotent in regulating the content of cigarette advertising on the air. According to the story Braren told the committee, as far back as 1966, a confidential study made by the staff of the Code Authority had found that a good deal of the cigarette advertising shown on the air depicted smoking as attractive and socially acceptable to young people in violation of its own standards. But the study had been ignored, Braren testified, and subsequently the resistance of the tobacco companies and the television networks made it impossible to police commercials. Braren said that when he and other Code Authority members suggested that the act of smoking be eliminated from commercials, "President Wasilewski intervened with the argument that such a proscription was 'premature,' that it would drastically reduce the appeal of cigarette advertising, and consequently not be of benefit to broadcasters." Then, said Braren, in 1967, Code Authority members were cautioned by the Code Review Board not to be "too rigid" in interpreting its guidelines by Board Chairman Clair McCollough, who told the staff that the standard in arriving at a decision as to specific commercials should be "When in doubt, O.K. it." Following an April, 1968, meeting of NAB officials to discuss the matter, according to Braren, review of cigarette commercials was virtually abandoned.

Stockton Helffrich, the Code Authority director, and Wasilewski denied charges that the NAB had been negligent in formulating and enforcing guidelines to govern cigarette advertising. Shocking as it had been, Braren's testimony had little effect on the House of Representatives, which voted by voice vote on June 18 for the committee bill. Every attempt to reshape the measure on the floor of the House met with defeat.

Pending Senate action, the FTC went ahead on July 1, 1969, with hearings on its proposal to require a health warning in all cigarette advertising. At those hearings, Dr. Luther Terry, the former Surgeon General, called the industry promise of voluntary self-policing a "complete flop." In fact, he said, the cigarette companies "get the youngest people you can see running up and down the beaches, frolicking." As for the industry-imposed ban against having sports heroes plug cigarette brands, Dr. Terry said the effect of that had been canceled by stepping up ad spots during sports events.

It had been predicted by some observers that one fine day someone would walk into Senator Magnuson's office and make him an offer. That day soon arrived. A delegation of broadcasters made him a visit in mid-summer and proposed a phase-out of advertising for cigarette brands with high tar and nicotine content. This proposal was conceived by network policy-makers in the Washington offices of the National Broadcasting Company on the theory that low-tar-and-nicotine cigarettes were less objectionable to the antismoking forces. Broadcast revenues also stood a chance of surviving under such a scheme.

To assist him in making a decision, the senator called on Michael Pertschuk, counsel of the Senate Commerce Committee, who had previously been an assistant to the then retired Senator Maurine Neuberger. In his mid-thirties, Pertschuk was a key figure in the congressional antismoking strategy and is given a large share of the credit for stirring Magnuson and his powerful Commerce Committee into action on a series of consumer-protection laws in recent years. Pertschuk sought the advice of Dr. Daniel

Horn, who told him that studies showed that although the low-tar-and-nicotine brands had some value for habitual smokers who were trying to shake the habit, in his opinion, the depiction of smoking on the air would offset any benefit from keeping the high-tar cigarettes off. According to the Horn studies, viewing the act of smoking can set back a smoker in his efforts to reform. But when all was said and done, Horn said the question was really one of morality. Was it right for the U.S. Government to accept promotion of a habit scientists believed to be seriously harmful?

The tobacco people were somewhat startled by the phase-out proposal of their friends, the broadcasters. And although Senators Magnuson and Moss rejected the scheme, they went on to exploit the uneasiness of the tobacco-broadcast alliance by pushing the broadcasters for further concessions in secret talks. A concession came with flabbergasting rapidity and totality. On July 8, the National Association of Broadcasters announced a plan to phase out cigarette advertising altogether over a period of three-and-a-half years, beginning January 1, 1970.

Senator Moss praised the broadcasters but asked, "Why must we wait four years?" The cigarette-makers reacted as if they had been touched by a lighted match. Already divided, they could now agree on nothing except their bitterness at what they considered a sellout by the broadcasters to whom they had given millions of dollars in advertising over the years. This was obviously the end as far as radio and television commercials were concerned.

The tobacco industry struck back with force. How would the broadcasters like withdrawal of all cigarette commercials at an even earlier date? On behalf of the nine major companies, Joseph Cullman, testifying at a July 22 hearing of Moss's consumer subcommittee, promised to end all advertising by September, 1970, if the broadcasters would release them from their contracts. There was just one string attached. That was a request that Congress grant the tobacco manufacturers immunity from the antitrust laws for making such a deal among themselves. This move was interpreted as leverage for new legislation needed by the industry to forestall the threat of state and federal regulation, including especially the threat of a health warning in advertisements.

The broadcasters were understandably aggrieved, having lobbied for the House bill favoring the tobacco industry. What galled them most was the thought that at least a sizable chunk of the more than $200 million that they had been getting annually for cigarette commercials would probably end up with their competitors, the newspapers and magazines. The broadcasters' reaction to the Moss suggestion was less than enthusiastic. All three networks turned it down. "If Congress determines that the permissive legislation sought by the Tobacco Institute is in the public interest, CBS will release the cigarette advertisers from their commitments," Dr. Frank Stanton, president of the Columbia Broadcasting System, wrote Moss. In other words, there would be no voluntary release. Dr. Stanton went on to ask the Senator: "If the public interest should require legislation in this area, should not the legislation deal with the problem as a whole and not direct its restraints only against the television and radio media? To put it another way, if the product is considered sufficiently dangerous to ban from one form of advertising, should it not be outlawed entirely?" American Broadcasting President Leonard H. Goldenson wrote that withdrawal of cigarette commercials "could well mean a substantial cutback in our news and public-affairs operations almost immediately and would also call for a complete re-examination of all other program commitments to see whether or not a full schedule of the present magnitude could be maintained. We do not believe that Congress would look with favor on any such forced curtailment of network service to the American public." ABC was then looking forward to tobacco-company sponsorship of the 1970 professional-football season with an asking price of $65,000 per minute for cigarette commercials run during the games.

In October, the Magnuson committee met in an atmosphere of recrimination. By then, the broadcasters had made several new moves. Wasilewski had complained to Moss in a letter that "there are indications that large sums of money would be diverted by the cigarette companies from broadcast advertising to promote their products by other means." According to this information, "vast expenditures would be made for promotional programs employing such devices as coupons, premiums, contests, point-of-sale promotion, and samples" as well as advertising in print. Rather than have Congress act on the tobacco companies' proposal, the broadcasters said they would prefer regulation by the federal agencies, which is what the tobacco industry feared most. At the same time, the tobacco lobby had been busy trying to get an extended pre-emption to prohibit the FTC from acting on a health warning in ads. Then, in a letter, tobaccoman Cullman placed his industry in a heroic, if astonishing, position by making it appear that if commercials continued on the air it would be solely because of the broadcasters' greed. NAB's Wasilewski responded by saying that the well-being of the broadcast industry necessitated a gradual, rather than an abrupt, end to cigarette advertising.

The FCC said it would be satisfied with a voluntary advertising blackout; its sister agency, the FTC, indicated that it would favor a strong health warning in other advertising, even if broadcast commercials were dropped. But the FTC agreed to suspend until July 1, 1971, its proposed order requiring such a warning. Senate strategists were now in an idyllic position. Senator Moss wrote letters to the networks suggesting that they release the tobacco companies from their advertising contracts.

On December 5, the Senate Commerce Committee voted out a bill banning cigarette commercials from the air as of January 1, 1971. Democratic Senator Philip A. Hart of Michigan had convinced the committee that it should not accept the terms of the tobacco industry's proposal to withdraw its advertising voluntarily in return for antitrust immunity. Senator Hart felt that such an antitrust exemption might prove a dangerous legal precedent for enforcement of the antitrust laws generally. The committee therefore settled for the statutory ban. The FTC was prohibited from acting on cigarette ads in newspapers and magazines until the middle of 1972. But a majority of the committee members said that they opposed this key provision, and Senator Moss threatened to filibuster against it; ten of the nineteen—including Chairman Magnuson—attached individual views to the committee report opposing the two-and-a-half-year moratorium on FTC action.

This topsy-turvy situation represented a new predicament for the cigarette-makers and the tobacco-state senators fighting to save the remnants of the victory they had achieved in the House. How had it come about? The eighteen-month delay had been adopted by a ten to nine vote. But Senator Norris Cotton (R., New Hampshire), one of the committee members who had expressed doubts, filed his own statement of opposition. Senator Moss now publicly stated that the bill would be "a giant step backwards" if passed. He cited an article in an advertising trade publication, *Media Decisions,* that predicted "the biggest switch of all times" when the TV ban went into effect. The magazine predicted that about two-thirds of the money cigarette companies had been spending on radio and television commercials would go into "alternate national ad media." The Senate bill called for a labeling provision weaker than the House-voted measure and a prohibition against cigarette regulatory action by the fifty states and local governments. The issue was not the sort that normally would have produced a successful filibuster. It remained to be seen what Senator Moss could do.

Magnuson and Moss took their fight to the floor of the Senate. In a night session on December 12, an amendment introduced by Senator Cotton and supported by Moss loosened the committee's proposed restriction on the FTC by allowing the agency to require health warnings in advertising as of July 1, 1971. The bill also authorized the FTC to move sooner if it found that tobacco companies were switching from broadcast to print advertising so massively that it could be considered a "gross abuse." Senator Moss also got the Senate to approve a new required health warning for cigarette packages—"Warning: Cigarette Smoking Is Dangerous to Your Health." The committee had proposed "Warning: Excessive Cigarette Smoking Is Dangerous to Your Health." By a vote of thirty-eight to thirty-five, the Senate knocked the "excessive" out of the warning. A number of tobacco-state senators joined the majority in the seventy to seven vote, apparently in the belief that even strong cigarette legislation would be preferable to no legislation with the FCC and the FTC waiting in the wings.

But that was not the end of the political maneuvering.

The measure still had to pass through the hands of a joint Senate-House Conference Committee, where important differences between the two bills had to be reconciled. The bill that came out of conference and was signed by President Richard M. Nixon on April 1, 1970, differed only slightly from the Senate measure. The cautionary label finally agreed on read, with governmental verbosity (and the problem of finding room on the package to print it in anything but rather small type) "Warning: The Surgeon General Has Determined That Cigarette Smoking Is Dangerous to Your Health."

In a final concession to the broadcasters, the conferees agreed to delay for one day the blackout of cigarette commercials from December 31, 1970, to midnight January 1, 1971. That would give them a last shower of cash from the New Year's Day football bowl games.

It also gave holiday viewers, most of whom had been unaware that the ban did not begin until midnight, one last, unexpected wallow in the sweet meadows of tobaccoland, through which young and beautiful blondes romped blowing cigarette smoke their way—or, if instant nostalgia was not the style in their family rooms, one last chance to curse their TV sets as commercial after commercial fouled up the airways and interrupted long passes.

♣ 14

Farewell to Marlboro, Salem, and All Those Country Places

THE EVE OF THE 1971 broadcast ban on cigarette commercials arrived amidst some confusion. The television networks reported receiving a flurry of telephone calls from viewers asking why all those ads were on the air. Curious but not angry, these viewers thought the ban was to go into effect on New Year's Day. They had forgotten, if they ever knew, that Congress, as a special concession, had given the tobacco companies an extra day to air their commercials. It was not until midnight of January 1 that the leathery-faced Marlboro cowboy rode into his last sunset.

All of the cigarette-makers spent heavily on their final TV fling. Philip Morris, Marlboro's maker, spent $1.2 million for commercial time between 11:30 P.M. and 12:00 on all three networks. Its twenty-five minutes during that half-hour included pre-midnight commercials on Johnny Carson's "Tonight" show, the Merv Griffin show, and the Dick Cavett show.

Some viewers saw the ban as a victory for the consumer. It gave them a welcome feeling of being able to influence the course of events. Others, on closing night, remembered radio's tobacco auctioneer, who concluded his ululation with the cry "S-o-o-o-oold American," Lucky Strike green marching off to war never to return, the diminutive page boy Johnny calling for Philip Morris, and agreed that these and some of their successors on TV had been Americana of the purest, brashest, wildly wonderful stripe. They would, they thought, probably miss them. Oh, not the ones in really questionable taste, of course. Or the irritating repetition of them.

Within the cigarette business, the obvious question was how the ad ban would affect the performance and marketing strategies of an industry as hooked on television as any smoker ever was on cigarettes. To hear some cigarette men talk was to marvel that the industry could survive at all. Milton E. Harrington, president of Liggett & Myers, told *Business Week* (November 21, 1970): "I feel our industry is at a more crucial point now than ever before." Richard H. Stinnette, assistant to the board chairman of American Brands, added that tobacco was a completely legal product, "yet no industry in the history of American business has ever had to undergo the kinds of pressures we are feeling."

Possibly the sorest point to come out of the ad ban was its expected effect on new brands that had been recently introduced. With more than 100 brands fighting for the consumer's attention, tobacco companies had relied heavily on television for a quick (two to three months), economical ($10 million) mass kickoff. Without television, brand introductions would take longer and cost far more. As TV's zero hour approached, tobaccomen rushed a slew of new brands to market. Reynolds went national with Vantage—for "every cigarette smoker who enjoys good taste but who's concerned about 'tar'." American Brands was promoting Maryland, a menthol variety. Philip Morris introduced New Leaf, also a menthol type, while Liggett

& Myers was distributing Eve, a cigarette for women, which was being promoted only through newspapers, magazines, and billboards to help gauge what cigarette-selling would be like under the broadcast blackout.

Where would all the cigarette commercials go once they had disappeared from radio and television? Most of them would go just where everybody expected—to the newspapers, particularly Sunday supplements, and to magazines and billboards. Long before cigarette commercials went off the air, the tobacco industry was busy using all its marketing genius to fill the void.

Because of the company's sheer size, the question took on special urgency for R. J. Reynolds, the nation's largest cigarette-maker. Ironically, it was the cancer scare that first helped Reynolds move into the lead (accounting for nearly one-third of the U.S. market). Its filter-tipped Winston, marketed in response to the 1953–54 crisis, was top seller at the end of 1970. Reynolds also ran up record sales and finished the year with two other of the six best-selling brands: fourth-ranked Salem and sixth-ranked Camel. Pretty good for a company that had been insisting for fifteen long, ungrammatical years that "Winston tastes good like a cigarette should."

As the industry's biggest ad spender, Reynolds had allocated fully 80 per cent of its 1970 ad budget to television. Another 10 per cent went to magazines, while the rest dribbled into newspapers, billboards, point-of-purchase displays, and other media. Once the ban went into effect, Reynolds cut its total ad budget some 25 per cent. What was left went into other media and some new promotions. To keep sales and profits rolling in, Reynolds took a look at its marketing program. At the field level, it strengthened its sales force. By the end of 1970, it had between 1,000 and 1,500 salesmen keeping tabs on its 400,000 outlets. The sales force was to play a more important role than it had during all the years television had carried a heavy selling load.

For some time, magazines had been expressing optimism about their prospects for new business. John T. Landry, a Philip Morris vice president, was quoted as saying that representatives from the advertising departments of various publications were going to tobacco companies as if to hear "the reading of the will." Senator Moss wrote letters to a number of publishers to sound them out on policy. Andrew Heiskell, chairman of Time, Inc., replied that "it would not be in the public interest or our own for us arbitrarily to refuse to carry the responsible advertising of a lawful product." Several magazines did not accept cigarette advertising as a matter of principle, notably *Reader's Digest,* the *New Yorker,* and the *Saturday Review,* but they were very much the exception.

There were also a few newspapers that did not accept cigarette advertising. The *Christian Science Monitor* had never carried it. The *Boston Globe* had announced in May, 1969, that it would no longer accept such advertising "because accumulated medical evidence has indicated that cigarette smoking is hazardous to health." After the tobacco industry decided to drop radio and TV ads, the *New York Times* announced that "in advance of the steps we hope Congress will take to establish tighter health safeguards by law, the *Times* is taking voluntary action to ensure that a health warning accompanies any cigarette advertisements it carries." As of January 1, 1970, the *Times* explained, the paper would accept cigarette ads only if they contained a health warning. The Tobacco Institute responded to this move with a full-page ad in the *Times* that explained in a headline "Why We're Dropping The *New York Times.*" The American Tobacco Company had "offered" to take its commercials off the air, the ad said, because of the "claim that those media unavoidably reach large numbers of children," and "not because we agree with anticigarette crusaders (including the *New York Times*) who would like to blame cigarettes for the thousand and one ills that flesh is heir to." The other major cigarette companies soon thereafter made known their intention not to advertise in the *Times* under the prescribed conditions.

Among their new promotions, the cigarette-makers were planning to sponsor auto races, a Canadian golf tournament, a bowling tourney called the Winston-Salem Classic, and a series of women's tennis matches called the "Virginia Slims Invitational." An urge to sell, not sporting blood, was obviously the motive. *Tobacco Reporter*, a trade journal, explained in its issue of August, 1970, that

> the advertising has been banned, but not the appearance of the product during the feature programming. For instance, at a stock car race one or more of the participating vehicles will have a cigarette promotion blurb on its side. In following the race the television cameras will pass fence advertisements while the crews and winners will be smoking with the cigarette pack prominently displayed. Such will hold true for any number of sporting events that appear on television. It could even go so far as to have the football booster section displaying block cards that promote a particular brand.

But as the hour of the broadcast ban approached, Senator Moss warned against "unconscionable hucksterism running amok within the cigarette industry." The Utah Democrat cited mass mailings of sample cigarettes addressed to "occupant," and the American Brands plan to name its pipe tobaccos "Pall Mall," "Silva Thin," and

"Tareyton," in packages similar to those containing their cigarette namesakes. Moss said the sporting events could also put cigarette promotion back on television despite the law.

Reynolds President, William S. Smith, took exception to reports that the purpose was to circumvent the broadcast ban and sent telegrams of denial to major newspapers: "The recent publicity in your publication and others attributing ulterior motives to our company's sponsorship of bowling tournaments, automobile races, and other popular spectator sporting events is completely without foundation and is but another example of the unremitting vendetta being waged against cigarette smoking."

Reports that tobacco firms were considering coming back on the air through the side door also alarmed some government officials. In a December 23, 1970, letter to President Vincent T. Wasilewski of the NAB and Horace R. Kornegay, the former congressman who was now the new president of the Tobacco Institute, the chairman of the Federal Communications Commission called attention to statements of Senator Moss referring to reports that preparations were under way to "subvert" the intent of Congress. FCC Chairman Dean Burch later called a meeting of these gentlemen to discuss the purported moves. In a news conference following that meeting on January 8, 1971, Chairman Burch said that the respective industries had pledged themselves to adhere to the spirit as well as the letter of the law and would avoid inadvertent television exposure of cigarette advertisements.

The news conference was enlivened by an exchange between Chairman Burch and anticigarette crusader John F. Banzhaf III, whose request to attend the meeting with Wasilewski and Kornegay was rejected. Banzhaf asked why representatives of the public could not attend a meeting that was of concern to them. He noted that Action on Smoking and Health (ASH), which he headed, had made some allegations in a formal petition for rule-making but was not invited to the meeting. "Doesn't this raise the suggestion you're really meeting privately with people you're supposed to be regulating?" Banzhaf asked.

Chairman Burch replied that, in an effort to resolve questions raised by allegations, he called a meeting of those "most directly" involved. If it had been a matter of formal rule-making, he would have done something else. "If you're suggesting we're out to make a deal," he said, "you're wrong."

"It raises the suspicion," Banzhaf shot back.

Meanwhile, on the sidewalk outside the FCC offices on Washington's congested M Street, three law students were parading with papier-mâché death masks trailing black shrouds and labeled "FCC, Cancer, Tobacco," to protest Chairman Burch's refusal to let ASH representatives into the meeting. To passersby, the students handed out a statement headed: "No more meetings in smoke filled rooms."

Following the cut-off date for broadcast commercials, a clear indication of trends in newspaper advertising was immediately evident. In their papers of January 4–7, 1970, the *New York Times* and *New York Post* each carried one cigarette ad. In the papers for the same days of 1971 they each carried nine. The *Chicago Tribune* carried sixty-five column-inches of cigarette advertising in its editions of January 5–7, 1970, and 170 column-inches from January 4 to 6, 1971. In comparable periods, the *Washington Post,* which editorialized vigorously in favor of the law prohibiting cigarette advertising on radio and television, published 119 column-inches in 1971, compared to fifty-six in 1970. Also, during the first week of January, 1971, Lorillard made an exclusive contract with Controlled TV Communications, Inc., of New York, to advertise its cigarette products via closed-circuit at race tracks throughout the country in 1971 at a cost of several million dollars.

Antismoking pressure from Washington showed no signs of letting up. The New Year had just dawned when Surgeon General Jesse L. Steinfeld warned that a pregnant woman who smokes creates risks for her unborn child. "As a result we are losing babies and possibly handicapping babies," he said in a January 11 speech. In making this statement, Dr. Steinfeld relied mainly on a British study of 17,000 single births—98 per cent of all births during one week in March, 1958, in England, Scotland, and Wales. For each 1,000 births, the rate of infants born dead was 27.6 for women who smoked, 19.3 for women who did not. The incidence per 1,000 of neonatal deaths (infants dying within the first four weeks of life) was 17.2 for women who smoked, 13.1 for women who did not.

Most drugs taken during pregnancy cross from the mother's circulation, via the placenta, to that of the fetus. The sleep-inducing drug thalidomide was a notorious example of adverse effects on the baby. If the mother is a morphine addict, the baby usually becomes addicted while in the uterus; after birth, the baby, unless given gradually reduced doses of the drug, usually develops withdrawal symptoms. Nicotine also passes into fetal circulation if the pregnant woman smokes. Usually, the habit may not be harmful, according to the report of the British doctors, though it may temporarily increase the fetal heartbeat. Their report said, however, that 18 per cent of the mothers who smoked ten or more cigarettes a day had children who developed convulsions in the first seven years of life, compared to 13 per cent for nonsmoking mothers. There were also ninety-three epileptic children, some of them afflicted seriously, among those of smoking mothers.

Later that month, the Surgeon General fired another salvo: a 488-page report to Congress describing new experiments further linking cigarette-smoking with heart disease. These studies in animals and humans showed that nicotine in cigarettes increases the work of the heart and its demand for oxygen, leading, said Dr. Steinfeld in his 1971 report (like the "Terry Report," published by the Government Printing Office), *The Health Consequences of Smoking,* to an increase in heart attacks among people prone to coronary disease. While other factors—including diet, obesity, and high levels of blood fats—are closely linked to fatal heart attacks, Steinfeld said that cigarette-smoking is an independent cause that can accelerate other risks. Besides causing the heart to work harder, the nicotine in cigarettes also stimulates the release of a chemical called catecholamine that causes an increase in fatty acids in the blood and might be the mediating factor between cigarette-smoking and thrombosis. According to the report, nicotine may alter the heart's rhythm so as to cause ventricular fibrillation, the wild, uncontrolled beating of the heart that is a common cause of death among heart-attack victims. Other cited studies suggested that cigarette-smoking may contribute to the clogging of the arteries that often precedes heart attacks.

According to Surgeon General Steinfeld, pipe- and cigar-smokers were not as safe as they had previously thought. In his report to Congress, Dr. Steinfeld said that because pipe- and cigar-smokers rarely inhale deeply, they are only slightly more susceptible to lung cancer than nonsmokers, but they can develop cancer of the mouth or lip. For the many pipe-puffers and cigar-chompers who do draw smoke down as far as the larynx, he said, chances of developing cancer there are three to seven times greater than those of people who avoid smoking.

The industry appeared to desire less discussion of the health controversy. Tobacco Institute President Kornegay predicted "sharply reduced noise levels" in the smoking and health debate, leading to a speed-up in the scientific process. The native of Greensboro, North Carolina, saw the "scientific findings" of the U.S. Public Health Service as little more than a high-priced publicity campaign. None of the findings, he argued, actually linked smoking with serious illness. Noting a slight rise in cigarette sales in 1970, the first in several years, Kornegay declared that "it is apparent that the American Cancer Society and other groups misjudged public gullibility." "The public," he added, "has total awareness that smoking may be a health hazard, but they demand the facts, not surmises. Not only are the thousands of lung-cancer victims who have never smoked cigarettes being neglected by expensive propagation of myths instead of scientific knowledge, but there are signs of a direct backfire." He also referred to a 1970 survey by the federal government's National Clearinghouse for Smoking and Health, which showed that the number of teenage boys smoking cigarettes had risen 25 per cent in two years and the number of girl smokers had gone up 42 per cent. "Cigarette companies don't want that kind of customer," he declared. "Years ago they quit campus promotions, stopped using popular heroes and youthful models in their advertising, so as to emphasize that smoking, like many other activities, is an adult custom to be decided upon by mature people." The Tobacco Institute chief reported that leaf companies would pool more than $4 million in 1970 toward scientific research on the health question, and, noting that 1970 was a record high year for the $10 billion industry, said, "I know of no single individual among the hundreds of thousands of tobacco farmers, manufacturing and distribution employees and executives and retailers who believes he is profiting from poison instead of pleasure."

But, for the cigarette-makers, new trouble appeared on the horizon and would continue to appear. First, a stiff health-warning in all cigarette advertisements and on the front—not the side—of all cigarette packs was recommended by the Federal Trade Commission. The commission also proposed a new law requiring disclosure of tar and nicotine levels in ads and on packs. Both proposals paralleled legislation promised by Senator Moss. Next, Representative William D. Ford (D., Michigan) responded to a letter from an angry constituent in suburban Detroit by introducing legislation that would outlaw all unsolicited mailings of cigarettes. Consumer complaints had been triggered by a flood of cigarette samples in several urban areas sent out by American Brands. Residents of Washington, D.C., Baltimore, Miami, Detroit, Southern California, Rhode Island, and the state of Washington had complained to congressional and postal authorities that they were receiving packages containing two packs of Silva Thins and Maryland 100's, with a printed commercial for the products. Offices of the attorneys general in California and Florida asked American Brands to suspend mailings in those states because minors had been reported receiving cigarettes in violation of local laws.

As the antismoking mood strengthened, Ralph Nader asked the Federal Aviation Administration to require separate smoking and nonsmoking areas on commercial aircraft. Although the agency turned down his request, some airlines voluntarily followed through on his proposal. (The new jumbo jets are big enough to allow the separation of smoking from nonsmoking passengers.) John Banzhaf started a campaign to segregate smokers in restaurants and government offices. "We are not unnecessarily infringing upon anybody's smoking pleasure," he said. "What we are doing is upholding the nonsmoker's right to be free of the danger and nuisance of other people's tobacco." Some of Banzhaf's students were preparing to ask the FTC to stop the use of regular cigarette trademarks on candy cigarettes sold to children. Others were compiling medical evidence to try to convince the Bureau of Narcotics and Dangerous Drugs that, for some people, tobacco is a physiologically addictive drug like heroin. Banzhaf was also preparing do-it-yourself kits for people who wanted to bring damage suits against the tobacco companies. (Probably no single specter so haunted the cigarette companies as the possibility of a flood of successful lawsuits by lung-cancer victims, which could bring jury awards rocketing into the millions and even tens of millions of dollars.)

The stamina of the tobacco industry was being put to the test. Success or failure depended on a handful of issues, among them the advertising controversy, overseas trade, domestic consumption, new promotional methods, research, and increased taxation. State and local taxes on cigarettes had skyrocketed in the past few years—in the view of industry executives, posing almost as great a threat to future sales as the health issue. In 1969, twenty states boosted levies on cigarettes and seven others followed suit in 1970. State taxes ranged from a high of 18 cents in Pennsylvania down to 2 cents in North Carolina. Cities and counties had also turned to cigarette taxes as a way to raise revenue. The tax imposed by New York City was 4 cents a pack. Kansas City and St. Louis had a 5-cent tax. The federal government, which had held the tax on cigarettes to 8 cents a pack since the early 1950's, took in $2 billion in fiscal year 1970, or $6 million a day.

For an industry in trouble, the cigarette-makers continued, however, to show remarkable vigor. They had no intention of abandoning the field. Despite the health controversy, profits were rising. Many investors agreed with security analysts who were optimistic about the prospects for higher profits, and stock prices were doing well. Projections of earnings were good even without the results of the tobacco companies' diversified activities. From a pack of Winstons selling in New York City for 53 cents a pack, roughly 15 cents went to the retailer and distributor and 27 cents to federal, state, and local taxes. Of the remaining 11 cents left over for the manufacturer, 7 cents went into manufacturing and shipping costs, and 2 cents into advertising and marketing. This left Reynolds with a pretax profit of roughly 2 cents a pack. Twice in the eighteen months prior to the ban on radio and TV commercials, the cigarette companies raised prices. These increases more than offset the higher costs of raw materials, packaging, and processing. Steady gains in manufacturing efficiency had trimmed labor costs in cigarette factories. The result was additional gravy in terms of profit margins.

A key question was whether a TV-less industry could recruit the new, young smokers it needed to sustain it. Tobaccomen claimed they could. Whiskey had never been advertised on television, they pointed out. Neither, for many years, had Hershey candy bars. Neither had marijuana. Tobaccomen also took solace in their industry's growing success abroad—where broadcast bans have long been in existence—and examined the foreign market for clues as to the long-range effect of their enforced withdrawal from Marlboro country. Despite a ban on radio and television ads for cigarettes in Britain, consumption rose in 1968 to 121.8 billion cigarettes—an increase of 2.7 billion over the year before. In Holland, which bans advertising of both tobacco and cigarettes, adults were smoking 1,433 cigarettes per head in 1968, up from 1,287 six years earlier. Although the Italians had clamped down on all tobacco advertising in 1962, total sales rose by about 17 per cent in the year 1968 alone. Abolition of price-fixing had helped boost consumption in Switzerland despite a complete advertising ban. Even behind the Iron Curtain, consumption was rising. In Poland, where advertising for cigarettes and tobacco is barred, Poles smoked 1,840 cigarettes per head a year in 1967, up from 1,790 the year before. (Consumption was also up in Austria, Spain, Sweden, Norway, Belgium, France, West Germany, and Yugoslavia, where advertising was permitted. In the Soviet Union, there is little advertising of any sort and no published statistics on smoking.)

Smoking American-blend cigarettes made of high-quality tobacco had become a status symbol to many people around the world; their consumption was rising rapidly in areas where the standards of living were rising. U.S. companies were putting heavier stress on foreign markets. Philip Morris, for instance, was marketing in more than 150 countries through export licensing or direct manufacturing. Reynolds had started making cigarettes in Germany and Switzerland in 1968 and planned to begin production in a new plant in Puerto Rico to serve the Caribbean.

At home, certain signs suggested that the all-American addiction to cigarettes might be turning to a new form— and substance. Roll-your-own cigarette papers had come to the cities and were sitting high in the saddle. Nationally, sales jumped nearly 400 per cent. The Internal Revenue Service, which levies a tax of half a cent on every package of twenty-five or more papers sold separately from tobacco kits, and keeps a careful tally on figures, says that sales stayed in a narrow range from 50 million packages of cigarette papers in fiscal year 1965 to 61 million in fiscal year 1969, with a drop to 45 million in 1967. Then, in fiscal year 1970, sales zoomed to 214 million packages. The old standard cigarette paper—the 10-cent Zig-Zag—had been joined by such exotics as Papel Paja de Trigo and Indio Rosa. There were flavors—sweet mint and cherry, banana, licorice, and chocolate—not likely to make tobacco taste better.

Most cigarette companies were refusing to accept the premise that increased use of marijuana was the major factor in the cigarette-paper sales boom. They claimed it stemmed from a growing number of people rolling their own tobacco. Milton Rothenberg, vice president for sales of the United States Tobacco Company (Sano, Mapleton, Stratford cigarettes), distributors of Zig-Zag papers, said that the rise in cigarette-paper sales reflected higher state taxes on manufactured cigarettes. A lot of people were using the new cigarette-rolling machines, according to Rothenberg. But Hank Bahrenburd of American Brands, manufacturers of Bull Durham, one of the more widely known tobaccos for rolling your own, said publicly that there had definitely been no significant growth in roll your-own tobacco sales by his firm. Department of Agriculture estimates tend to support Bahrenburd, although sales of cut leaf, the kind that is generally used in homemade cigarettes, were up a little in Kentucky. There were persistent rumors that the tobacco industry was planning to go after the pot trade, but the cigarette-makers sternly denied such talk.

In the course of 1970, chewing tobacco had been enjoying a steady growth as cigarette-smoking came under increasing attack from the health interests. The quid had been there all along, of course, moving up and down in popularity as it did between the jaws of men (and a few women) who favored it. To the conquerors of the New World, the aboriginal American custom of chewing tobacco was abhorrent, but gradually the habit was taken up in Europe. Pepys referred to the prophylactic value of a "chaw." Students at Dutch and German universities in the eighteenth century debated the supposed therapeutic value of chewing tobacco. The clergy, unhappy that indiscriminate chewers made the floors of churches unsanitary for kneelers, appealed to their congregations to desist from its use. Readopted by Americans, chewing tobacco became part and parcel of the wide-open days of the frontier. "Set right there, stranger, an' I'll jest miss ya!" was the tobacco spitter's friendly remark in hotel lobby or saloon. "Even steady old chewers of great experience were not always good marksmen," wrote foreign visitor Charles Dickens, "which has rather inclined me to doubt that general proficiency with the rifle of which we have heard so much in England." The condition of the Senate carpet drew distressed comment from Dickens, who also told his readers: "Washington may be called the head-quarters of tobacco-tinctured saliva. . . . In all the public places of America, this filthy custom is recognized. In the courts of law, the judge has his spittoon, the crier his, the witness his, and the prisoner his." The U.S. District Court in Washington authorized a ban of the cuspidor from all federal buildings in 1945. Nobody was agitating for the return of the spittoon in 1970, but chewers of plug, twist, and scrap tobacco (and some new twentieth-century dippers of snuff) were saying that they got an economical and quick lift from their chosen products while keeping their hands free for work—and their lungs of smoke.

Against all this background, and despite all their strength, there was a continued broadening of activities by the cigarette-makers into lines far removed from tobacco as a way to keep profits growing. Tobacco was still king. After two straight years of decline, cigarette consumption in 1970 moved up to slightly more than it had been in 1969, though it still stood far below the 1967 record. But it was obvious that manufacturers wanted a hedge against a possible eventual serious drop in cigarette consumption.

Since 1964, American Brands, the country's second-largest cigarette manufacturer, had bought five companies. In 1970, it agreed to buy Andrew Jergens, the manufacturer of skin-care preparations, and Master Lock Company, a privately held manufacturer of padlocks. Between 1963 and 1970, Reynolds laid out $200 million for diversification. In 1969, in one swoop, it spent another $530 million for Sea-Land Services, Inc., a pioneer in the containerized shipping field. In November, 1970, it was awaiting government approval of a $65 million deal—for acquisition of U.S. Lines, Inc., a subsidiary of Walter Kidde & Company, a natural complement to Sea-Land Services. American Brands in 1970 had acquired two office-equipment manufacturers. Philip Morris had been discussing with the Weyerhaeuser Company the purchase of a paper mill in Michigan. Liggett & Myers was the most highly diversified company, with 43 per cent of its sales coming from nontobacco sources. Like Reynolds and American Brands, Liggett & Myers had dropped the tobacco from its name. In 1970, it bought full-page ads in the nation's daily press to ballyhoo that "Liggett & Myers, the tobacco company, has become Liggett & Myers, the pet food, liquor, wine, cereal, popcorn, watch band, and tobacco company."

♣ 15

A New Leaf?

EASTWARD FROM RALEIGH, NORTH CAROLINA, the rolling terrain and red clay of the piedmont give way to the flat fields and dark loam of the coastal plain, the most productive tobacco country in the world. Through the winter, nobody, except perhaps the Florida-bound motorists, pays much attention to the plant beds lying idle, plastic sheets covering countless patches of dark, sandy soil. To the tourists, the beds and curing barns that dot the countryside are simply curiosities. Sometime between mid-January and early March, depending on the location and weather, the plant beds will be seeded, the plastic covering stripped away and replaced by cheesecloth. Planting time comes in mid-May, so in early spring, the shoots will be plucked gently from the bed plants and transplanted, symmetrically —forty-two inches between rows, twenty-two inches between plants—into the dark loam. By early summer, when the leaves begin to ripen, rows of Bright leaf will cover some 580,000 acres of land from southern Virginia to northern Florida and the tip of Alabama. Another 217,000 or so acres of Burley will stand ripening in the hills and bottom lands of Kentucky, Tennessee, and western North Carolina.

Tobacco has always been a demanding crop, requiring large amounts of hand labor and some skill in its growing and curing. "No sick child demands more constant and careful watching than a barn of the golden leaf when it is being cured by the flu[e] process," one chronicler said more than half a century ago. The harvesting of the Bright leaf, the flue-cured variety that makes up about 50 per cent of cigarettes, requires more labor than Burley, and a vast army of field hands, most of them black, are still tied to the crop. Altogether, more than half a million farm families in eight states look to the tobacco crop as their major and, in many cases, only source of income.

In the long debate over smoking and health, the tobacco farmer has been largely forgotten. Ever since the Surgeon General issued his report in 1964, the giant tobacco manufacturers have played the role of defender of the industry —and villain to the reformer. But even if they lose the battle for public opinion, the cigarette companies can take care of themselves. They will weather the storm. If Americans stop smoking, it will be the thousands of farm families, dependent on tobacco, who will pay a hard price.

Like other people, tobacco farmers watch television. These days, they don't like what they see, or rather don't see. The lack of cigarette commercials disturbs them. The government has hit where it hurts most, and they're afraid the ban on cigarette commercials will put them out of business. You can't tell them cigarettes may be harmful to health. They don't believe it. Furthermore, they think the money the government is spending trying to kill the cigarette habit is a waste. Bitter remarks are exchanged about the "quacks" in Washington. Wishful thinking about the health issue still prevails among farmers who hope the American Cancer Society will lose interest in its "I Quit" crusade and that the "health scare" will turn out to have been a bad dream.

Feelings run strong in tobacco country. John Rolfe's golden leaf created a class of small, yeoman farmers, men whose tiny patch of tobacco gave them an essential freedom. Today, many tobacco farmers are third generation or even more. Tobacco has been a way of life to them, and they are prepared to defend it.

In Kentucky, in the winter of 1969–70, Burley farmers decided to fight back in their own way. At auction houses across the state, they chipped in $1 each to finance a lawsuit in the U.S. District Court in Lexington by eight of their number against the three national television networks. The eight farmers who were plaintiffs claimed that they had been damaged by the antismoking commercials aired by the TV networks—both because farm real estate with tobacco allotments had declined in value and because tobacco prices had dropped. The farmers' lawyer, Robert Odear, wanted to silence the more provocative ads, like the one showing a smoker's head rolling off. "It's never been proved that cigarettes are killers," Odear said. "If they say that cigarette smoking might be injurious, we don't challenge that. But when they come out with a flatfooted statement, it's ridiculous." State Senator Tom Harris, who runs a Burley warehouse at Carrollton, Kentucky, said, "The big companies used to do the battling. Now the people are scared and they're mad. They want to see what they can do."

Statistics on smoking give little solace to the farmer. There are signs that the long effort to educate the public to the potential dangers of smoking is finally paying off. In 1966, 51.9 per cent of all American men twenty-one or older smoked cigarettes. In 1970, according to government estimates, that figure dropped to 42.2 per cent. For women, the comparable figures were 33.7 per cent in 1966, down to 30.5 in 1970. The consequences of the smoking-and-health issue were beginning to show.

But even before Americans in really sizable numbers stop smoking, if they ever do, even before the seed is scattered down the plant beds this year and next, hundreds of tobacco farmers will know that this crop is their last. Thousands more will be wondering how much longer they can hang on—because today, tobacco, agriculture's last great stronghold of hand labor, is in the early stages of a double revolution, sponsored, not by government nor private health agencies, but by the tobacco industry itself.

Since the mid-1950's, manufacturers have reduced the quantity of leaf in a cigarette by an average of 2 per cent a year. During the 1960's, use of flue-cured tobacco dropped by 15 per cent, for a market loss of 100 million pounds. By 1969, use of Burley had dropped almost 6 per cent. Growers blame among other factors (and they are quite correct in this) the consumer shift to filter brands, which have captured about 77 per cent of the cigarette market. Filter-tip cigarettes have a shorter tobacco column than most non-filter brands. Also, new technology permits manufacturers to use the stems of tobacco plants, parts once thrown away, thereby further reducing demand for the more expensive leaf portion. There is a growing trend, too, toward "thin" cigarettes as well as toward use of imported, low-nicotine tobacco for blending purposes.

Until recently, tobacco economists in both tobacco belts had generally assumed that, if present trends persisted, it would mean steady consumption of tobacco for the next decade or so, or at worst, a modest decline. Either, by itself, would squeeze out thousands of farmers as operating costs continue to rise and the market remains stagnant or slackens. But now farmers are shuddering at the possibility that demand for tobacco will shrink dramatically even if cigarette sales hold their own. Under development are two new processes to expand the volume of tobacco—"freeze-drying" and "puffing"—which means that manufacturers will be able to buy and use far less leaf per cigarette.

In mid-November of 1970, Reynolds announced that it had devised a process to expand the shredded leaf, increasing the volume of a given weight of tobacco 40–50 per cent. A Reynolds spokesman has said that "tests conducted to date indicate that puffed tobacco would account for a relatively small percentage of the total tobacco blends used in Reynolds brands." But the *Wall Street Journal* has reported that Reynolds plans to switch to exclusive use of puffed tobacco in its cigarettes over the next couple of years. Other tobacco manufacturers and researchers at North Carolina Agricultural Experiment Station in Raleigh are working on a freeze-drying process, which also has about twice the filling capacity of conventionally processed tobacco.

A cigarette with half as much tar and nicotine might cool off the health critics, North Carolina Governor Bob Scott told alarmed farmers when they found that their own state university was developing a freeze-dried process. He also suggested that the new process might lead to greater use of flue-cured tobacco in blends. Burley growers had been smug about the "health scare," on the theory that cigarette-smokers would turn to pipe tobacco, which relies heavily on their leaf. The 1970 output of smoking tobacco rose to 69 million pounds, a five-year high and an over-all gain of 9 per cent over the year before, but cut tobacco for roll-your-owns accounted for the increase. Pipe tobacco remained unchanged.

The Department of Agriculture is spending some $5 million for tobacco research, about $2 million of which is aimed at making cigarettes better tasting, better smelling, and better looking—more desirable to the consumers. The other $3 million goes for research that is considered health related. Dr. E. L. Moore of the Department's Plant Industries Station at Beltsville, Maryland, says that while his goal is to produce tobacco more suitable to market demands, that does include the elimination or modification of any objectionable constituents in tobacco leaves. "We can develop various levels of nicotine, if it seems this is what the consumer demands," he says, adding that tobacco with a nicotine level below a certain point is not tobacco. "The consumer uses tobacco for whatever pleasure he gets out of it, and probably nicotine is part of it."

Nicotineless cigarettes produced some years ago failed on the market. The movement now is toward cigarettes containing less tar and nicotine, not "safe" cigarettes, according to Public Health Service officials, just "less harmful" cigarettes. But research sponsored largely by tobacco manufacturers has also developed cigarettes that look, taste, and smell like the real thing but do not contain a shred of tobacco. Celanese Corporation has announced that it is working on a synthetic tobacco for the future, containing the same basic material used in cigarette filters, cellulose acetate. Apparently, domestic manufacturers have no present plans to market nontobacco cigarettes because of the lack of data on what effect the substitute materials might have on smokers' lungs. Part-tobacco cigarettes, identified as containing a substantial quantity of nontobacco ingredients, are sold regularly in the United States by foreign manufacturers.

Although exports of tobacco products have reached record highs in recent years, they have failed to offset a decline in exports of tobacco leaf. U.S. exports of unmanufactured tobacco in 1970 totaled 510 million pounds, 12 per cent below 1969. Major markets, the United Kingdom and several European countries, took less than in 1969. U.K. cigarette-manufacturers reduced over-all imports and also shifted to lower-cost sources, including a number of developing nations that have moved vigorously into tobacco production. Salisbury in Southern Rhodesia now handles more tobacco than any marketing center in the United States. (It it just one more irony in the long story of tobacco that sanctions by the United Nations against Rhodesia, imposed because of its apartheid policies, should benefit U.S. tobacco-growers. The U.S. Government, in upholding the U.N. embargo against Rhodesian exports, was probably not unmindful of the joy such action would bring to Tobaccoville, U.S.A.) Higher U.S. prices and the improved quality of tobacco produced in several developing countries in Latin America, Asia, and Africa have so increased competition in world markets that U.S. exports will do well in the decade ahead to hold at the 1970 level.

American tobacco-growers are also faced with the necessity of producing tobacco free of pesticide residues if they want to maintain their overseas market. West Germany, which, as the second largest foreign market for leaf exports, over the two years 1968–70 purchased 95 million pounds valued at $85 million, took action that resulted in a ban on DDT-use on tobacco crops and requires tobacco-growers to meet a January 1, 1973, deadline for an extremely small tolerance of pesticide residues on tobacco. Other European purchasers of U.S. tobacco were expected to follow the West German lead.

But as the 1970's began, the export situation was just one of many factors driving U.S. tobacco-growers to cut production costs. Although returns on tobacco are good, rising production costs have been eating into much of the increased profits. The traditional, almost ritualistic methods by which tobacco has been grown, harvested, and marketed can no longer prevail against recent technical and scientific developments—and the need for cheaper leaf.

The old system survived because it had available the strong backs of hundreds of thousands of laborers—poor whites as well as Negroes—who were offered little more than bare survival in the near-feudal system. The relatively few big planters relied on tenants and sharecroppers to produce the crop. Small landowners and, frequently, tenants themselves have depended heavily on impoverished blacks, paying them modest wages during the brief harvesting season but giving little more than free housing (usually of the sorriest sort) the rest of the year. This layered society has been shaken in recent years as blacks and poor whites have moved out of the tobacco fields in increasing numbers. Some of them have been replaced by ever-more-advanced machinery rumbling into the fields.

Some small tobacco-growers in the Southeast are taking land out of production because, they say, it is impossible to get labor, and their farms are not large enough to warrant the expense of mechanization. Crops in parts of Maryland went to waste in 1969 because of lack of help. Some larger farmers have resorted only recently to importing migratory labor. In the central tobacco-growing areas of North Carolina, a combination of high school students, migrants, and others usually can be scraped together to help with the harvest, but it is becoming more and more difficult. North Carolina's first tobacco labor-camp was built in 1969 in Wake County.

In Wilson County, North Carolina's largest flue-cured-tobacco-producing county, the curing barns stand in clusters of five or six. Rows of collard greens grow beside the tenant cabins where the black people live. There, the changing economics of agriculture and the awakening of the southern Negroes have reduced the number of farmers during the last twenty-five years or so from some 4,300 to about 1,400. Bill Lewis, the county's agricultural-extension agent, figures that the number of farm operators will drop to 500 in the years ahead. From his perspective, the "health scare" is just one more calamity. The time will come, he believes, when farmers will either have to get big or get out. Lewis is proud of how farmers have branched out in the last ten years, a trend typical of North Carolina as a whole. The local incomes from sweet potatoes, hogs, cucumbers, eggs, and milk have increased. Yet, tobacco still means about $20 million a year to the county. "There is no panacea," says Lewis. "If there were any other crop good enough to replace tobacco, Wilson County farmers wouldn't be the only ones growing it. They'd be growing it in Washington, D.C."

In Bright country, each tobacco allotment carries with it a corresponding quota stipulating the maximum number of pounds of leaf that can be marketed. In the past, many farmers found that they could rent their allotments and clear about as much profit as they could by farming the acreage themselves. But since 1967, the rental market has dropped sharply because of the high cost of production, cutting in turn the price the farm can expect in rental. In 1968, 72,000 acres of tobacco were rented in North Carolina at an average price of about 14 cents per pound on an average quota of 1,800 pounds, or a return of about $250 per acre to the owner of the allotment. Allotment owners by the thousands have been learning that their allotments or portions of them are nearly worthless. North Carolina bankers also report that the price of land for growing flue-cured-tobacco allotments has declined. In 1965, land carrying flue-cured-tobacco allotments sold for $5,000 to $7,000 an acre. In 1969, it was selling for $3,000 to $4,000. The decline was attributed to the labor situation.

In the bluegrass country of Kentucky and in the surrounding shale belt with its comparatively rough topography, the principal cash crop is Burley. One reason tobacco has long been a favored crop in Kentucky is that it is profitable to raise on any size farm. Most farmers, even dairymen, require thirty to forty acres of good cropland or meadow to make a bare living. But the Appalachian tobacco farmer can get by if he can raise the food and livestock for his own needs, plus a few acres of tobacco for money. In the Burley belt, for instance, more than 55 per cent of the farmers have tobacco allotments of only one-half acre or less, a tiny plot that produces as much as $1,000 or $1,200 a year—the only cash that many hillside farmers in eastern Kentucky and Tennessee see all year long.

In the Burley belt, while farmers are producing more tobacco every year because of chemical fertilizers and pesticides, consumption is not holding. In 1970, Burley use dropped by 2 per cent, though buyers found the crop usable and bought rather heavily. The year before, when prices had dropped alarmingly, a record amount of Burley had been passed over by buyers from the cigarette companies and thus had to be purchased by the government-financed price-support "pool."

Government price support is mandatory for all kinds of tobacco produced under marketing quotas. The price support reflects a rise in the parity index, which is a measure of changes in prices paid by farmers, wages paid to hired labor, interest, and taxes. Support levels for the 1971 crop were up 4 per cent over the year before. Since tobacco normally is aged several years before use, the companies can let the surplus sit in the government pool until they need it. They can then buy it from the pool at the bargain interest rate of 3½ per cent, much more cheaply than at current interest rates in the commercial money market.

To the ominous assumption that the cigarette companies

are taking a businesslike hedge against the uncertainties of the future, farmers add their worry that the government will not keep on buying tobacco nobody wants, that the Department of Agriculture will drop the program of price supports, which brought price stability to tobacco markets historically so chaotic that there were once barn-burning insurrections among discontented farmers. The government-financed surplus stocks of tobacco in 1971 totaled 1.2 billion pounds packed weight worth about $1 billion.

It is quite understandable that farmers have begun to wonder whether such government underwriting can survive. If the supply-and-demand relationship changes radically, tobacco price-support programs cannot function smoothly. If tobacco consumption goes up, the government is repaid for its investment. If it turns down, the government gets stuck. Farmers, who have already taken acreage allotment reductions and, in Bright country, poundage quota reductions, too, cannot endure repeated reductions to compensate for reduced consumption. They wonder how long the government will maintain supports for the crop in the face of proposals that tobacco programs be phased out. From the perspective of Washington, the problems may not seem insurmountable. But the way farmers see it, Congress's almost annual threat to drop the support program seems to pick up new converts every year.

If government programs were eliminated abruptly, it would be the cigarette companies and large growers who would benefit. Milton Shuffett, a University of Kentucky economist, estimates that if the government dropped acreage restrictions, Burley farmers would grow too much tobacco and prices would drop about 25 per cent in the first season. The large growers might survive several years of poor prices, but thousands of small farmers would be shaken out of the tobacco economy. In the Carolinas and other flue-curing states, tobacco farms are generally larger and more often in the hands of a commercial operator. But there, too, the potential for social fallout is great. In North Carolina alone, it has been estimated that 100,000 farm families will be surplus labor by 1975. Most of these families are black.

Some farmers are turning to other crops. They talk earnestly about crops ranging from cucumbers to soybeans to blueberries to wine grapes. "I'm sure we can increase these things, but they are not going to pick up the slack for tobacco," says Charles Gulley, county extension agent for Fayette County, Kentucky, the prosperous bluegrass horse-farm and tobacco-growing area surrounding Lexington. Less resourceful or less realistic growers are not looking in new directions. Tobacco is what they learned from their daddies and what they are teaching their sons. Some small landowners, those who hold allotments of three to five acres, are selling out as tobacco farmers—sometimes to take industrial jobs that are beginning to open up in the region, more often to remain on the land as truck farmers or chicken farmers.

One replacement crop that the farmers in central Kentucky could easily grow, if it were legal, is marijuana. Across the bluegrass region, farmers joke about marijuana's competition with tobacco. Oddly, before tobacco took over, the principal crop in the region was Indian hemp—grown for rope. What the farmers call "voluntary hemp" still flourishes uncultivated along fences and creek beds. The sheriff of one central Kentucky county caught some young people harvesting it on his own farm.

Some steps are already being taken to revise government programs to allow for an orderly reduction in the amount of tobacco produced and in the number of farmers who produce it. The first tentative proposals are beginning to surface. In North Carolina, for instance, the Farm Bureau has suggested government payments for farmers who want to retire their allotments. Early in 1970, a congressman from the mountains of southeastern Kentucky, Republican Representative Tim Lee Carter, put forward his own version of a "soil-bank" program for retiring Burley acreage. "It may cost quite a bit of money," Carter said, "but we've got to do something."

For a great many tobacco farmers, it does not really matter whether the upheaval comes in a single season or gradually over a decade. The Negro tenants and sharecroppers have little hope of surviving on the land, no matter how gradually the revolution progresses. Thousands of them are leaving the tobacco fields every year, unable to survive on the tenant's share of a five-acre patch or less. Their departure for the urban centers of the Northeast has created a labor shortage affecting larger tenants and small landowners, speeding up mechanization, and thus creating more pressure on the marginal operators to get out or get bigger.

Despite the difficulty of putting together large tobacco operations, the trend is clearly in that direction. Mechanical harvesters already are operating on a few large farms. Once the demand for such machinery is sufficient to justify commercial production, the harvesters will sweep the small landowner and the tenant right out of farming. It requires no great imagination to foresee the day when a relatively few large corporate farms will grow all of the flue-cured tobacco the market demands. The corporate farms might even grow it on contract to the manufacturers.

What science and technology did to the cotton fields of the Deep South and to the coal fields of the southern Appalachians is now being repeated in many other places, and with distressingly similar results. Especially in con-

temporary agriculture, workers are being displaced from
their livelihoods. Where can these rural refugees go but
to the already overburdened ghettos of the cities? Even in
Asia, where to make the so-called Green Revolution work,
the new hybrid cereal seeds were given to the best farmers,
with the result that the big farmers have succeeded and
driven the small farmers out, cities are being inundated
by the newly jobless in scenes reminiscent of the black
migration to American cities during the major mechanization of Southern agriculture in the 1950's. If current
projections hold true, the economic squeeze in world agriculture is likely to produce a gradual kind of agony, especially painful for the thousands who already live on the
tattered edge of subsistence farming. For the United States,
and especially for the marginal producers in America's
oldest industry, it could mean new waves of dispossessed
mountaineers or black farmhands following the migratory
path to the cities. In a statement in April, 1969, former
Virginia Governor Mills E. Godwin, Jr., noted that the
"illustrious history" of tobacco has included the provision
of "employment for millions." Tobacco, he said, "has paid
ministers of the gospel, financed educational institutions,
sponsored millions of dollars of medical research and contributed greatly to underwriting the cost of federal, state,
and local governments."

Never no more?

Some hard choices are involved in deciding who gets
hurt and who survives in tobaccoland. Does the government seek economically viable farm units or the social
objective of maintaining income for the rural poor and
stemming emigration?

Among the men who still raise the fragrant leaf named
for Jean Nicot, talk runs to the upheavals of our times,
the steady exodus of black people from the South, the

minimum-wage law, the new harvesting machinery that reduces labor needs, the textile mills that are drawing away their remaining field hands. Small farmers all over the United States have gotten used to seeing general prosperity pass them by. But for tobacco farmers the future looks especially bleak. They think that everything is stacked against tobacco.